WOMEN of the CIVIL WAR

by Darlene Funkhouser

Dedication

This book is dedicated to the memory of my parents, Austin and Millie Funkhouser -- a fine Virginia gentleman and a true Southern belle.

Acknowledgements

I would like to sincerely thank the following people who aided me greatly in the writing of this book:

-- The patient librarians at the Lady Lake, Florida library: Mary McIntyre, Rebecca Winfield (thank you for the family Civil War story), and Joe Nitto, a true wizard at finding research sources;

-- My publisher and editor, Bruce Carlson for his knowledge and his sense of humor, and his wife Marilyn who keeps him in line;

-- The following folks who graciously sent pictures and historical details of plantations: Julie Rowe (Boone Hall), Nancy Roberts (Destrehan), Anna James (Longwood), Christine Gaudet (Madewood), Jane Taylor (Magnolia Plantation and Gardens), Trey Castleberry (Oak Alley), and Randy Carter (Shirley);

-- The following friends: Ellie Anderson who suggested that I get serious and start to write, Anne Bardelli for her encouragement, Dr. David Bonnett for accompanying me on many trips to battle sites (and for taking some excellent photographs), Debbie, Mitchell and Merrick Egber for always being there through thick and thin, Midge Maddison for her enthusiasm, Stephen Rabbito who has patiently listened to every step of this book, Joe Shadrick for his awesome sense of humor, and Andy Starliper for his compassion and his delightful sense of humor.

Table of Contents

Introduction

Women played an important and an often underrated part in the Civil War. While men marched off resolutely to fight in the first modern war, women found themselves thrust into unfamiliar, sometimes unwanted roles. Suddenly, they were factory or office workers filling spots left vacant by their menfolk. Often, they kept these spots open for their men. Other women had to learn how to manage farms or run the business aspects of plantations. Others became shopkeepers hoping to keep family businesses running until the men came home -- if they did.

The majority of women had children, so the unrelenting pressure was on to feed those hungry mouths and to keep a warm roof over the children's heads. Military pay was sometimes slow in coming, and it could not be relied on to arrive home in time.

To aid the war effort, women rolled bandages and sewed uniforms, and they raised money for supplies and medicines. They volunteered at hospitals and wrote letters home for soldiers. They gave wounded, scared young men warmth and companionship, and they sometimes cradled men as the brave soldiers slipped away.

The roles taken by ordinary, everyday women were not all that surprising. Women have performed similar functions in all wars -- they have kept the home fires burning while hoping to see the faces of their loved ones again. The more unusual female undertakings are the subjects of this book. Within its pages, you will read about the two steely first ladies of the War Between the States.

Female soldiers were perhaps the bravest of the Civil War women. Most disguised themselves as men. Most eluded detection for the duration of their service; some did not. When their gender was detected, interesting things would often happen. Their reasons for fighting in a war in a time when women were not in the services are varied and touching.

Women were successful spies for both sides. While their secret work sounds exciting and somewhat romantic, it was actually fraught with peril and danger. It is difficult to imagine what would drive someone to take up spying. If caught, a person would be charged with treason and could be put to death.

Women in the medical field played a vital role. There was one physician, Dr. Mary Walker, who was way ahead of her time by becoming a doctor in the first place. That was not a typical feminine profession in those long ago days. Nurses had tough duty under the most extreme conditions -- the battlefield. On that front and in hospitals, nurses' abilities and mettle were tested time and time again.

Abolitionists were an important force in bringing the nation's attention to the horrors of slavery. Women were an integral part in this battle for basic human rights and dignity.

Harriet Tubman played a dangerous role before and during the War. She was responsible for transporting many slaves along the Underground Railroad. By all accounts, she was unafraid of danger and exhibited no personal fear.

Other famous women live on in these pages -- women whose names and stories will forever be a part of the rich fabric of our great, enduring American history.

Southern Belles at
Auburn Plantation
Natchez, Mississippi

Lovely, graceful hoop skirts
were worn during the Civil War, and our
Northern sisters wore them as well.
Although hoops were somewhat collapsible,
imagine the difficulty in mobility that
would occur in closed areas at parties or
in church!

The Two First Ladies

America has always had a special fascination with its first ladies. After all, one would assume it would take a larger than life woman to catch the eye of a man destined to become a president! First ladies must wear many hats. They serve as role models and as ambassadors for the United States. They plan, arrange and help preside over state dinners and other formal functions. They must be aware of the customs and traditions of other countries both when they welcome foreign guests and when they are guests in other countries.

First ladies are steady workers of charitable and philanthropic causes, and most adopt a specific way to help keep our nation strong. Some have encouraged greater literacy, while others have championed welfare reform or improved health care and other social concerns.

American women look to first ladies as arbiters of style, often copying hairstyles and fashions. First ladies sometimes generate great excitement during their tenure. Miss Frances Folsom married President Grover Cleveland in 1886 in a spectacular White House wedding. Details of the nuptials were consumed by a rapt nation.

First ladies must be consummate hostesses, often being gracious in trying situations. They must be intelligent and savvy about domestic and world affairs. They tend to stay in the background, allowing the president to do an often impossibly difficult job and offering support as he does it.

It is a life lived somewhat in a fishbowl, and this was never more apparent than during the Civil War. Miss Mary Todd Lincoln and Miss Varina Davis were in the spotlight of two nations during a long, ghastly war, and neither would fare all that well.

Mary Todd Lincoln

Miss Mary Todd was born into wealth and privilege on December 13, 1818 to Robert and Eliza Todd, pioneer settlers of Kentucky. When Miss Todd was six, her mother died and her father remarried. She went to finishing school at age fourteen, and she received advanced education at the age of nineteen. She was pleasingly plump, her eyes were very blue, and her hair was light brown. She was a true, vivacious Southern belle who used her considerable wiles. She adored parties, balls, dinners and finery.

When almost twenty-one, she was sent to Springfield, Illinois to find a husband. Living with her married sister, Miss Ninian Edwards, Miss Todd happily fell in with a group of lively young people who called themselves "the coterie". The group were interested in politics, literature, romance, parties, excursions, dances, balls, and picnics. The group most often gathered at the Edwards' fine mansion.

Mr. Abraham Lincoln, in contrast to Miss Todd's pampered life, rode into town with all his worldly possessions in two saddlebags. Also born in Kentucky, he would rise from a hardscrabble frontier childhood in rural Indiana and Illinois to ascend to the highest rung of the political ladder. Along the way, he worked on farms, operated a ferry and was a flatboatman who traveled to bustling New Orleans. In spite of scant childhood schooling, he learned surveying, served in a war, managed a general store and was admitted to the bar in 1836. Now thirty years old, he aimed to make a name for himself.

When presented to the belle at a cotillion, he said, "Miss Todd, I want to dance with you in the worst way". After the dance, holding her bruised dancing slippers, she laughingly told her cousin, "And he did". Cupid's arrow took a wavering path. There was a stormy three-year courtship, a broken engagement, and a period of separation. She was immature and in some ways never grew up. She was excitable and made no attempts to hide what she was thinking or feeling. Mr. Lincoln, of course, was as solid and steady as an old mule.

In the end, he was quite tolerant of her high-strung ways, and they married at her sister's house on November 4, 1842. Her wedding ring was engraved with the words "Love Is Eternal".

Her early married life in Springfield was lived in greatly reduced circumstances to which she was unaccustomed, having been raised with servants. The newlyweds started their life in a boardinghouse called The Globe Tavern where meals were taken in the common dining room. They paid four dollars a week for rent, and first son Robert Todd Lincoln was born there in August of 1843. The young Lincolns soon bought a house of their own. The family grew by three more sons -- Eddie, Willie and Tad. By now, Mr.

Lincoln was a successful lawyer.

Miss Lincoln was not physically well and pregnancy, unfamiliar household drudgery, headaches and childbirth were starting to wear on her. Adding to her mental strain was the sorrow she felt over the February 1850 death of toddler Eddie. He had fallen ill and died almost two months later.

She was forced to be both mother and father to her children because Mr. Lincoln was a circuit judge for six months of the year. In his lifelong desire to help people, he rode to the furthest reaches of the circuit. Theirs was a lively household with pets (he loved cats, while his wife was less enamored of them), toys and happy, roughhousing children always underfoot.

Her mental instability developed gradually. If she was having a fit of anger in private and could not appear publicly, sad-eyed Mr. Lincoln would say she was having one of her nervous spells. Or, he might say she was not well that day. She suffered excruciating headaches, which would now be called migraines, which often confined her to her bed for days at a time.

Miss Lincoln had lofty ambitions for her husband. They went to Washington, D.C. for his single 1847-48 term in Congress. They returned to Springfield where Mr. Lincoln continued his law practice. He was elected President in 1860. He was totally surprised, but his wife knew all along that he was destined for greatness. Her unflagging faith and gentle nudging allowed him to realize his full and considerable potential.

She was roundly criticized for her extravagant spending in the White House. She redecorated the Executive Mansion into a model of splendor. She was spending government money, and her lavish taste and her searches for "only the best" soon exceeded the appropriated money. An amount of twenty thousand dollars had been allotted and she overran that by seven thousand dollars in 1860 dollars. Now forty-three years old, she became known for her finery in clothing as well, and she made frequent shopping trips to New York City.

She opened the White House lawn to the public on Wednesday and Saturday evenings in nice weather when the Marine Corps Band played. She was criticized for having the usual receptions and dinners in time of war, then she was criticized when she did not.

She was very jealous of her husband, and she did not like White House etiquette that said she could not march at his side at official receptions. She said she was his wife and should lead with him. She did not like the thought of him walking with another woman. After a time, she either walked with him or he marched alone or with another gentleman.

Her fellow Southerners scorned her as a traitor to her birth. This scorn was unfounded because she had a brother, three half brothers and three brothers-in-law serving in the Confederate States of America Army. That fact did not appease Southerners. Northerners, on the other hand, thought she might be practicing treason by passing military information to the South.

Son Robert avoided the fishbowl life of the White House; he was at Harvard during most of the Presidency, but he came home for vacations. His little brothers Tad and Willie were rambunctious and happy. Once, strong Abe Lincoln was helplessly pinioned to the floor by the lads and two playmates. The boys were proud of themselves for being able to restrain the tall man! The White House roof did double duty at various times as a circus ground, a fort, or the deck of a ship. The boys also made a theater in the house. Willie was Miss Todd's favorite child.

When he became seriously ill at the age of twelve, his mother did not willingly leave his bedside. With his 1862 typhoid fever death, the sunshine went out of her world, never to fully return. She was unable to go to his funeral, and she never again entered the room where he died. She curtailed her lavish entertaining because of her grief. Then, people said she was shirking her duties as First Lady.

That summer, she felt well enough to visit soldiers in the hospitals. She did this privately, choosing not to have reporters around. Her heart was good, and she did a lot of charitable work.

In an attempt on the President's life, screws on his carriage were loosened at the Gettysburg battle. Miss Lincoln was thrown from the carriage, hitting her head on a sharp rock. Son Robert felt she never fully recovered from the nasty head wound.

She did not get to hear the President deliver the Gettysburg Address because she was at home with an ill Tad. She was, by this time, an abolitionist and she was in full support of her husband's missions of preserving the Union and freeing slaves.

She was totally irresponsible about money and spent willingly on herself even as war casualties mounted. She used an enormous amount of credit (who could refuse the First Lady?), and she ran up huge debts. Mr. Lincoln knew nothing of her increasing debts, and she panicked wondering how she would ever pay them.

For the second inaugural ball in March 1865, she wore a two thousand dollar white silk gown with an elaborate headdress. She purchased along with the gown a thousand dollars worth of mourning clothes. Perhaps she was spooked by her husband telling people that the war was killing him and he would never live to see peace.

On the lovely spring afternoon of April 14, 1865 -- Good Friday -- the Lincolns went for a happy drive together alone. The President talked freely of what they would do once his term was up. He thought they would go abroad; he especially wanted to see Jerusalem. They continued their pleasant time by going to Ford's Theater later that night to see the play, Our American Cousin.

At 8:20 that night, they entered the flag-draped box at the theater. When John Wilkes Booth's bullet hit the President, Miss Lincoln felt his hand go limp in hers. She screamed and fainted. After a long night of anxious prayers, President Lincoln died that morning.

Miss Lincoln could not go to their bedroom and was taken to a guest room.

She remained in the darkened room for five weeks, alternately shrieking, shuddering and weeping. She could not go to his funeral and said years later that she had no recollection of the weeks after his death. She was utterly devastated by her husband's death. Gone was her solid rock and the gentle, steadying presence who loved her no matter how excitable she became. Gone was her staunchest supporter who stood by her through the public's unfair, petty criticisms.

She traveled abroad with Tad for six years. They wandered from city to city, staying in cheap lodgings. She received a portion of the money President Lincoln had left, around forty thousand dollars, but she soon ran aground financially. She tried to sell her fancy gowns in New York, but the sale did not go well. The public was aghast that a former president's wife would resort to such measures.

She petitioned Congress and received one year's presidential pay which amounted to twenty-two thousand dollars. She eventually received a small annual pension of three thousand dollars which was later raised to five thousand dollars. In January 1882, Congress voted her a donation of fifteen thousand dollars.

She and Tad returned to America in 1871 to see her new granddaughter. Tad died at the age of eighteen shortly after their return, and her fragile mind slipped further. She thought people were trying to poison her, and she shopped, shopped, shopped. She was rapidly dissipating her estate, so Robert stepped in and had her declared legally incompetent before she could fritter away everything.

She was committed to a mental institution for four months, then she was released to the care of Miss Edwards until she was judged normal. She went to France for the next four years. In late 1879, she fell while trying to hang a picture, and she was partially paralyzed over the lower part of her body. She came back to America to Miss Edwards' house and made up with her son. She sought help from an orthopedic surgeon in New York and came back to Springfield in an invalid's chair.

On July 16, 1882, she fell unconscious and died. She died in the house where she was married forty years earlier. It is where she optimistically began a new life with a remarkable man who many feel may have been the greatest president America has known. It was a tragic, yet fascinating life that would take her much further than lesser women could ever hope to go.

Varina Davis

Miss Varina Anne Howell was born on May 7, 1826 in Natchez, Mississippi at The Briars. She received a fine private education complete with finishing school. Her paternal grandfather had been governor of New Jersey from 1793-1801.

At seventeen, she met Mr. Jefferson Davis during Christmas, 1843 at Mr. Davis' brother Joseph's plantation thirty miles south of Vicksburg. She was smitten with the thirty-six-year-old widower whose first wife, daughter of Zachary Taylor, died three months after the wedding. At 5'10", Miss Howell was almost as tall as he. Dark-haired with almost black eyes, she was a commanding presence even as a teenager. They married in 1845 when she was nineteen.

Mr. Davis hunted alligators and he could be lighthearted, but he tended to brood. He was not socially outgoing, so his wife shored up that part of their marriage. She ran his house, re-arranged furniture, gave the place a woman's touch, sewed and rode. She read about politics, law and business. Mr. Davis was not in good physical health. He suffered from nervous tension and had much trouble with his eyes. His wife would spend a lot of time doctoring him.

They soon went to Washington, D.C. when he was elected to Congress.

Politicians found her shrewd, witty and a good listener; men liked to engage her in serious conversation. The Davises lived in a boardinghouse. Miss Davis acted as his secretary, writing, reading and researching on his behalf.

During his term, he went off to fight in the Mexican War against her wishes. He was wounded and became a national hero. The Davises were comfortable but far from affluent. She was a dollar stretcher by necessity; her planter father had never made a good living. She grew up reasonably well, but her mother always had to economize. Mr. Davis sometimes helped the family financially.

Back in Mississippi, their planter's life took on a comfortable sameness. Then, they got a tremendous shock. After almost seven years of marriage, they were to be parents! Samuel Emory was born in 1852, and the family moved to a brand new house, Brierfield.

The Davises moved back to Washington, D.C. in 1853. There, they rented a house, and Miss Davis did her own housekeeping for the first time. They quickly became a part of the White House circle, and Miss Davis became a social leader. She was fashionable but not chic. She never had a large wardrobe, and her jewelry was sparse and simple. Fond of white, she had an easy elegance. She knew how to gracefully end conversations with people she considered boring or slow-witted. She could be sarcastic, and she was direct and got right to the point.

She suffered through her husband's ill-fated camel experiment. He thought the creatures could be well used in the

American desert. Thirty-three were imported for thirty-three thousand dollars in 1855. They, being dirty, spitting animals were turned loose by Army personnel whenever possible. Camels were not as hardy as mules, and horses did not like them and created a fuss. The remainder were auctioned off, and a few wound up in circuses.

In the summer of 1854, two-year-old Samuel died. That fall, his parents moved to their permanent home; the house had twenty-three rooms and quickly became a celebrity hangout. Margaret Howell was born in February 1855, and brother Jefferson followed in January 1857.

In 1857, Mr. Davis was active in the Senate. Abolitionists were in overdrive, peppering Congressmen with propaganda. The Davis family toured New England that summer. Southerners felt the Davises were being traitors. By the end of the decade, many Southern politicians gathered quietly at night in the Davis parlor. Son Joseph Evan was born in April 1859.

In January 1861, storm clouds gathered as Mississippi was set to leave the Union. Mr. Davis left the Senate and before reaching Mississippi, he was appointed a major general of the CSA Army. On a balmy spring day, the Davises were making cuttings of his beloved Glory of France rosebushes. A messenger galloped up with a telegram informing Mr. Davis that he had been chosen to be President of the new nation. Mr. Davis was surprised and upset; his wife knew he would have much preferred to lead the Army.

He left for Montgomery, the original capital of the Confederacy. Miss Davis was in Natchez during his inauguration; she was thirty-five when she arrived in Montgomery and gave a reception the night she arrived. She returned to Brierfield to bring back furniture and children.

She became renowned for her hostessing abilities. Richmond was chosen as the new capital, being much closer to the Northern capital. Miss Davis arrived in June 1861, and she liked her new three-story showplace home. She cut back on entertaining; some people called her extravagant, while others thought her stingy. A fourth son, William Howell, was born.

She regularly visited hospitals with supplies. She also knitted for soldiers along with sister Maggie who had come to keep her company. Miss Davis was used in 1863 by Judah Benjamin, Secretary of State, to carry state papers disguised as letters. She used assumed names for her espionage stint; the letters were seemingly innocent but were written in code.

Tragedy struck in April 1864 when five-year-old Joe fell off a railing and died. Miss Davis was stoic as the Confederacy began to crumble. She slowly disposed of things -- books, china, silver, art, furniture. She made twenty-eight thousand dollars and had it converted to gold.

She left Richmond with the children and Miss Maggie at the end of March 1865. Living in the woods, they headed to Florida. Richmond fell, and the Davises were now fugitives. Separated, husband and wife exchanged messages by courier. He was going to Florida to be taken by boat to Texas.

They were reunited, but his aides advised him to leave to avoid capture. He said he would take a meal with his family, then leave. Two Union detachments were in the woods unaware of Mr. Davis' presence. He put on his wife's waterproof, and she threw her black shawl over his shoulders. They hoped he could escape through the early morning mists. The Yankees noticed the "old woman" was wearing boots, and "she" was captured.

The trunks were broken open, and the gold was confiscated. Miss Davis and her party were taken prisoner and marched to Macon. She eventually wound up jailed in Savannah where she knew no one. She sent her children to Canada with her mother, but kept baby Winnie with her.

Now free, she wrote letters on her husband's behalf. In May 1866, she had a prison reunion with him at Fortress Monroe, Virginia. She and Winnie would be allowed to spend short periods of time with him. She made a quilt that told the story of the Confederacy -- her "immortal patchwork" that was a record of better days.

Mr. Davis was released after two years, and the Davises immediately went to Canada and lived in Quebec during the summer of 1867. Mr. Davis was without a country because he would never sign an oath of allegiance to the United States.

They went to Cuba that winter because his fragile health could not withstand the harsh Canadian winter. They left Cuba after Christmas and went to New Orleans, then back to Canada. Mr. Davis took a job in Liverpool, and they took rooms in

Dorset Square in the spring of 1869. They visited Paris for a few weeks that autumn. Miss Maggie married dashing Chevalier Charles de Wechmar-Stoess; they would have a daughter.

Mr. Davis' business venture failed, and he was offered a position as president of a life insurance company. He found his job difficult -- it was simply a way to support his family. Son Billy died at age twelve of diphtheria in 1872. The insurance company failed, and Mr. Davis again sought employment.

He embarked in 1874 on a bitter family lawsuit to regain Brierfield. His brother Joseph had gotten the plantation back in 1866 by taking the oath of allegiance and receiving a pardon. He would not give his brother title to Brierfield, so the younger brother sued to get back what was rightfully his. Four years later, Brierfield belonged to Mr. Jefferson Davis.

In 1876, Miss Margaret returned to America and married Mr. J. Addison Hayes, a young banker. The marriage made national headlines. The Hayes later moved to the frontier town of Colorado Springs.

The Davises returned to England for a business venture that failed. Now close to seventy, he decided to write a book. Miss Davis was not immediately able to accompany him back to America. He moved to Beauvoir, a gracious Mississippi house on the Gulf Coast that would be his final haven. A friend, Miss Sarah Dorsey, invited him to stay there while he wrote The Rise and Fall of the Confederate Government.

In autumn 1877, Miss Davis sailed

home but went to Memphis to console Miss Hayes who had lost her first baby. Mr. Davis came to see her and found she did not want to live on the Gulf Coast. She much preferred bustling city life to a tranquil one of watching the sea. Miss Dorsey threw a party in honor of the absent Miss Winnie who was in England. Miss Davis went to Beauvoir for the soiree and found gossip swirling about Mr. Davis and the widow Dorsey. By mid-summer 1878, Miss Davis had moved to Beauvoir.

Young Jefferson Davis was struck by yellow fever in October and died within a week. At twenty-one, he was the fourth of the sons to die. His mother went to Memphis to be with her daughter. Miss Dorsey, dying from cancer, transferred ownership of Beauvoir to Mr. Davis. He was to pay her five thousand, five hundred dollars in three installments. It came to light that she had willed Beauvoir to him. He paid the whole amount to her estate even though he did not have to.

Beauvoir was a wonderful home for the Davises, and they both worked on his book which took three years to complete. It was not a commercial success, but Mr. Davis did not care. In the tradition of Southern gentlemen, he had written it not for profit but as a history tome.

In 1881, Miss Winnie came from Paris to live at Beauvoir, and she loved living on the Gulf Coast with the beautiful water vistas. There were many visitors -- reporters, governors, generals, diplomats, and celebrities, including Mr. Oscar Wilde, and a train station was opened at Beauvoir. The Davises lived in quiet dignity at the water's edge. Miss Varina

Davis was often seen on the streets of Biloxi driving her little carriage pulled by her sprightly horse, Gladys.

The family had revenue coming in from properties they owned. Miss Davis' china was Staffordshire, and she treasured a cup and saucer that had belonged to Lord Byron. She had a hall mirror and console brought from Paris in 1871 that had belonged to the first Napoleon. The family prized a quilt stitched by three hundred and fifty Confederate women during Mr. Davis' presidency.

In the spring of 1886, twenty-two-year-old Miss Winnie was honored publicly in Atlanta. In Syracuse, New York, she fell in love with young lawyer Mr. Alfred Wilkinson. Miss Davis did not feel he would be able to support her daughter well. Miss Winnie sailed to Europe brokenhearted in the autumn of 1889 as she realized the South was against her for wanting to marry a Northerner. She had a nervous breakdown in December when she learned her father had died.

The Davises were married forty-four years when he developed bronchitis while away on business. Miss Davis rushed to New Orleans and nursed him. He died on December 7 at the age of eighty-one. He was dressed in Confederate gray, and thousands filed past his casket at City Hall. A Confederate flag covered the coffin along with flowers from Beauvoir.

Miss Davis started to write Memoir, her autobiography. She sent Mr. Wilkinson to Venice to see how Miss Winnie was getting along. He found her ill, and she came home in mid-summer. Her mother's meddling into her fiancée's family's financial and personal business ended the engagement; he would never marry.

Miss Davis went to New York City in 1891 to correct proofs and to meet with publishers. Over a period of three months, she had a succession of heart attacks, and Miss Winnie went to help her. Memoir never found its audience.

Miss Winnie had received Beauvoir from her father, but both she and her mother thought of moving north. For a year, they meandered between New York and Mississippi. Finally, they decided they could not afford to keep Beauvoir. Southerners were angry at them for living in the North.

In New York, Miss Varina Davis hosted Sunday salons at the Marlborough House where literary figures gathered. She wrote articles for the Sunday World newspaper for which she was paid a handsome salary. Miss Winnie wrote magazine articles, and she published two novels, The Veiled Doctor and A Romance of Summer Seas.

In 1893, Mr. Davis' body was moved to Richmond for final burial as tattered Confederate flags waved. Miss Davis trembled and lowered her head as the coffin was lowered.

Now sixty-nine, she moved to the Gerard Hotel in the heart of the theatrical district. In 1898, Miss Winnie sailed for Egypt after making a will bequeathing Beauvoir to her mother. She returned and died September 18, 1898 of malarial gastritis at the age of thirty-three. Mr. Wilkinson came to her funeral.

Miss Davis continued her newspaper assignments and kept up a large correspondence. Her tea hour became fashionable, and was a character of sorts. The Sunday World sometimes called her "Our Southern Queen"; she bore an uncanny resemblance to Queen Victoria. She attended musicales at the Waldorf-Astoria, and she liked afternoon tea, rides, cards, novels and a good bit of gossip.

In 1902, she toured Jackson, Vicksburg, Natchez, Memphis and New Orleans, and receptions were given for her by the United Daughters of the Confederacy. She sold Beauvoir to the United Sons of Confederate Veterans for ten thousand dollars. She was offered nine times that amount for it years earlier but would not see it become a hotel. It became a veteran's home.

At the age of seventy-seven while in Canada, she penned a five-page booklet called The Grasshopper War. It was a charitable fundraiser based on the war between the Huron and Iroquois Indians.

Miss Davis moved to The Majestic after fifteen years at The Gerard. She was excited because the new rooms would overlook Central Park. While moving, she developed pneumonia. She lingered for ten days; Miss Hayes hurried from Colorado before her death. Miss Davis died October 16, 1906 at the age of eighty.

Many mourned her death. President Roosevelt sent a wreath, and the Daughters of the Confederacy sent a heart of lilies and roses. Miss Davis was honored with a military funeral in Richmond. The woman who stood by her beleaguered husband through thick and thin was buried next to him on a hillside near the James River.

Shirley Plantation
Charles City, Virginia

Shirley Plantation, located between Richmond and Williamsburg, is Virginia's oldest plantation and the first built on the James River. Eleven generations of the Hill and Carter families have lived there, and current residents are descendants of the original owners.

The plantation has a colorful and illustrious history. During the Revolutionary War, Shirley Plantation served as a supply center for the Continental Army. It was also a listening post for both sides as our infant country struggled to break from England.

During the War Between the States, its many lovely rooms were turned into a Union hospital. The house was spared destruction by Union gunboats because of the hospitality shown wounded Yankees.

A square-rigged flying staircase rises three stories with no visible means of support. This marvel of engineering is the only one of its kind in America.

The plantation had another unusual design -- the spacious two-story kitchen.

Shirley Plantation is famous in the history of the Civil War because of an event that occurred there after Miss Anne Hill Carter married Governor Henry "Light Horse Harry" Lee, a fiery Revolutionary War hero, in the parlor. Their son was Mr. Robert E. Lee. He would later be faced with an important decision when asked to be a general for the Union after serving with the United States Army for thirty years. After much agony and soul searching, Mr. Lee chose to become a leader of the Confederate States of America Army. He said he could not go against his country; he was a Virginian

through and through, and he cast his lot
with the Confederacy.

The grounds now occupy eight hundred
acres, and Shirley Plantation has been
designated a National Historic Landmark.
Tours are given daily with the exceptions
of Thanksgiving and Christmas.

Women Soldiers

More women than people would imagine fought on both sides of the War -- a total of four hundred is estimated. A very few fought openly alongside men, sometimes participating in battle. These women often followed husbands or sweethearts. Most females fought disguised as men, and their reasons for fighting were probably the same as those of their male counterparts -- belief in their country, to escape the boredom of farms or small-town life, to see new places.

Women's duties on the battlefield were to carry ammunition and water, to provide medical assistance and to act as couriers between troops and their commanders.

Vivandieres or "Daughters of the Regiment" were a small but vital part of the war effort. These women did not fight, nor were they disguised as men. They sometimes acted as color bearers, and they kept up the men's morale by helping to write letters home and providing a sympathetic ear. They helped around camp wherever they were needed.

As for women who actually fought disguised as men, they were able to do so because there were no extensive physical examinations in those days. A cursory look at the eyes and ears and a listen to the heart and lungs were all it took to be tossed a uniform. Women bound their breasts to not show prominently, and one could never underestimate the advantages of loose-fitting clothes. Fireworks often erupted if someone's true gender was revealed -- varying consequences would be the punishment.

The stories of some of the brave young women who served their country in a most unorthodox way follow.

Malinda "Sam" Blalock

"Sam" Blalock and her husband Keith had an unusual war experience after they hatched a strange scheme. They were North Carolina born, but they were strong Union sympathizers. They joined the 26th North Carolina in April 1862 in order to be able to desert to the Union Army.

Miss Blalock disguised herself as a man, and her superiors noted that she did a soldier's duties as well as anyone else. The Battle of New Bern had been fought when the Blalocks joined, and the armies were now far apart. The Union Army had gotten out of easy reach.

With their plan of easy desertion thwarted, Mr. Blalock decided he could not remain in the Confederate Army. Seeking an honorable discharge, he rolled around in poison sumac. Presented thus to the Surgeon, he was granted a discharge.

Miss Blalock wanted to leave with him but found the idea of being covered with sumac boils unappealing. She told her commanding officer she was a woman. He did not believe her so he called the Surgeon over for an examination. The doctor told the Colonel that "Sam" was in fact, a woman. She was sent home with her husband three weeks after they enlisted.

Feeling a strong connection to the North, they felt they could still help the

North, they felt they could still help the Union. They got together a band of marauders and set off to terrorize denizens of the northwest North Carolina mountains. They raided the farms of loyal Confederate families, blithely being cocks of the walk until cruel fate stepped in and ruined their fun.

Late in 1863, they thundered onto the Moore family farm, shooting, shouting and generally acting crazy. The Moores shot back. Mr. James Daniel Moore was recuperating at home from a wound he received at Gettysburg, and he most likely did not appreciate the Blalocks' devotion to the Union. As a member of the 26th North Carolina, he had recruited them into his unit. Miss Blalock was wounded twice in this shoot-out.

Either stubborn or stupid (or both), the Blalocks sulked and licked their wounds for a while. Then they raided the Moore farm a second time. This time, the Moore boys shot Mr. Blalock's eye out.

The Blalocks decided after that to pick their targets more carefully. They participated with different Union forces during incursions into the mountains near the end of the War.

The Blalocks returned home after the War. Mr. Blalock made an unsuccessful run for Congress in the 1870s. Miss Blalock died in 1901. Life's ironies were not yet done with her husband. He died in 1913 at the age of seventy-seven. It seems he was pumping a handcar on a mountain railroad when he overshot a curve and fell off the mountain.

Sarah Emma Edwards

   Miss Sarah Edwards was born in Nova
Scotia in 1842 and tried mightily to
please her difficult father who had wanted
a son. She acted like a boy, hoping to
escape his wrath, but she finally left
home because of his abuse. She came
across the border and settled in Flint,
Michigan.
   The call for Union enlistments went
out, and she wanted to fight for her
adopted country. She cut her hair very
short and obtained a set of men's clothes.
She now called herself Frank Thompson and
was in the Army after four enlistment
attempts. She became a nurse on April 25,
1861 in the Second Volunteers. She should
have been on stage because her ingenious
performances were worthy of a theatrical
career.
   She trained in Washington, D.C. and
was sent to General McClellan's Virginia
campaign. She was assigned as a male
nurse to the hospital unit of the 2nd
Michigan Volunteers. Right before the
campaign began, one of General McClellan's
spies got caught, so Private Thompson
volunteered to act as a spy.
   Private Thompson decided to
infiltrate the Confederacy as an African-
American man for the first mission. She
used silver nitrate to darken her skin,
and she wore a black minstrel wig. She

choose the name "Cuff" and went behind Confederate lines. She was assigned to work on ramparts being built by local African-Americans to counter General McClellan. She convinced a slave to swap duties with her after the first day. Now working in the kitchen, she learned a lot of information. She learned about the Army's size, weaponry, and she found out about "Quaker guns" -- logs painted black to look like cannons. The Quaker guns were to be used at Yorktown to try to deceive the Yankees.

She returned to her own camp and met with the General who was well pleased with her data. She went back to nursing for a couple of months until her next assignment came; this one almost cost her her life.

In another performance worthy of the stage, she entered a Confederate camp dressed as a heavy-set Irish peddler named Bridget O'Shea. She sold some of her wares and gathered a lot of information as she floated around camp that day. This time, the Confederates chased her as she left their camp. They shot and wounded her in the arm. She almost fell off the horse she stole from the Confederates and later named "Rebel" but managed to thunder back into camp.

Her unit was transferred to the Shenandoah Valley -- "the breadbasket of the South" to participate in General Philip Sheridan's campaign. She meandered into Confederate camps several times as "Cuff". In August 1862, she went into their camps as a black mammy and became a laundress. As she was cleaning an officer's coat, a packet of official papers fell from the pocket. She returned to her camp, and the officers delighted in the information she provided.

Near the end of 1862, her unit was sent to General Burnside near Louisville. Her spy efforts continued at the new location. She was now Charles Mayberry, a man with Southern sympathies. Her task was to identify the spy network in Louisville -- a town in a border state. The mission was a success.

Her unit now went to Vicksburg under General Grant's command. Private Thompson was working in a military hospital when she contracted malaria. If she was examined at the military hospital, her gender would be revealed. She left camp and was treated at a private hospital in Illinois.

Now recovered, she planned to once again masquerade as a male soldier. While strolling in town, she read Army bulletins in a post office window. She was listed as a deserter! Her days as a spy who had accomplished eleven successful missions were over. She bought a train ticket to Washington and worked as a female nurse until the War was over.

She wrote her memoirs titled <u>Nurse and Spy in the Union Army</u>. It was a popular book that sold thousands of copies. The kind-hearted woman gave all her profits to the United States war relief fund.

Homesick for her native country, she returned to Canada. In 1867 at the age of twenty-five, she married Mr. Linus Seeyle. They moved to Cleveland and had three sons. Her sons no doubt were dazzled by her exciting war tales of danger and espionage.

As happy as her life was, there was still one fly in the ointment -- she still brooded over being labeled a deserter. She petitioned the War Department for a full case review. On July 5, 1884, a special act of Congress validated her, and she received an honorable discharge. She also received a bonus and a veteran's pension of twelve dollars a month.

Perhaps craving more agreeable weather, she moved to LaPorte, Texas in the late summer of 1889. She was eventually buried in a Texas military cemetery.

Jennie Hodgers

In July 1862, the President called for thirty thousand more men to serve in the Union Army. Miss Jennie Hodgers, 19, wanted to serve her country, so she dressed in men's clothing and went to enlist. After becoming PFC Albert D.J. Cashier of the 95th Illinois Infantry Volunteers, her unit was sent to serve under General Grant in Kentucky.

The 95th traveled over almost ten thousand miles of Confederate soil during the next three years. During the Battle of Vicksburg, Private Cashier was captured by rebels. She seized a guard's gun, knocked him down and made it back to camp. The 95th was honored at a public reception when they returned home.

Private Cashier settled in Saunemin, Illinois in 1869. He held many jobs -- church janitor, farm worker, lamplighter, handyman. No one suspected he was a woman. In November 1911, he was doing an odd job by picking up sticks in the drive of Illinois State Senator K.M. Lish. The Senator backed over him accidentally.

Dr. Ross, the Senator's friend, said that Mr. Cashier had broken a leg. The examination also revealed that Mr. Cashier was a woman. He pleaded with the men to keep the secret. The men thought he should have care at the Soldiers and Sailor's Home in Quincy, Illinois. At the age of sixty-eight, Mr. Cashier was admitted to the hospital as a male.

The secret came out when he applied for a pension increase. A sanity hearing was ordered, and the press got wind of it. He was now mentally feeble and was totally unaware that the secret was out.

In 1913, he was committed to the Watertown State Hospital for the Insane. He was housed in the women's ward and had to wear a dress for the first time in over fifty years. He died at the hospital on October 10, 1915. He was given a military funeral dressed in uniform, and the gravestone reflected his male name.

Miss Hodger's early life was a mystery. Born in Clogher Head, Ireland, she said she came to America as a stowaway or as a "male" cabin boy. No one knew for sure when she came to America.

On Memorial Day 1977, the townspeople had a new gravestone made for their little soldier which reflected both names. Flowers are placed on the grave every Memorial Day.

Loreta Velasquez

Miss Loreta Velazquez was a beautiful, fiery character who liked the limelight and money. She was the daughter of Cuban immigrants, and she eloped with an army officer in 1856. They had three children, all of whom died before the end of 1860.

When the War broke out, she wanted to enlist as a man, but her husband emphatically told her "no". She dutifully waved goodbye as he left in the summer of 1861. As soon as he was out of sight, she went to New Orleans. There, she cut her hair, bought a uniform and a mustache and was now Lt. Harry T. Buford.

Being of a determined set of mind, she mustered the Arkansas Grays, over two hundred men. She presented the unit to her husband for his command; he was far from pleased. He was soon tragically killed in an accident.

Broken-hearted, she left her troops and headed out. She participated in many battles including Bull Run, but she decided to leave the service. She turned next to spying, and she also smuggled supplies, correspondence and medical drugs. She was a Confederate soldier and spy for four years.

She thought her exciting war experiences were guaranteed page-turners, so she penned a book called <u>The Woman in Battle</u>. It received much criticism, but Miss Velasquez did not mind. She made no secret of the fact that she was only interested in selling as many copies as possible.

Sarah Rosetta Wakeman

Miss Rosetta Wakeman and her family did not hold out much hope of her getting married, and a future as a domestic worker held little appeal. A farmer's daughter, she dreamed of having her own farm some day. She was independent-minded, and she relished the idea of making a fulfilling life for herself.

By mid-1862 at eighteen years of age, she figured that earning a living as a man would give her more employment opportunities and earn her far more money. She dressed as a man and went to work as a boatman on a New York canal.

She wrote many letters home and told her family that some soldiers had encouraged her to enlist. Swayed by a one hundred and fifty-two dollar enlistment bonus, she signed up. Her Army time would, she hoped, enable her to someday buy her farm.

She enlisted as Private Lyons Wakeman in Company H of the 153rd New York State Volunteers. That October, the regiment headed to Alexandria, Virginia where it would perform police and guard duties to protect Washington, D.C.

Her lively letters home continued. She told her family that she was thinking of re-enlisting for five years to get an eight hundred dollar bonus. She was convinced that her unit would never see combat. She was proved wrong in late February 1864 when her unit was sent to Louisiana. A week or two later, the usually cheerful woman ominously wrote that she did not ever expect to see her family again.

On April 11, 1864, she saw combat at Pleasant Hill, Louisiana. She wrote that she was under fire for about four hours. In May, she was hospitalized for chronic diarrhea. She managed to escape detection because medics could tell she had diarrhea and did not feel the need to examine her.

She died on June 19 and was buried in a military ceremony with no one the wiser as to her true gender. Her identity came to light a century later when her letters home surfaced -- she had signed them "Rosetta".

Cathay Williams

Miss Cathay Williams was not a soldier in the Civil War, but she later played an exciting part in America's history. Born into slavery in 1842 in Missouri, she was a house servant. When the War began, the plantation was taken by Union troops. Miss Williams and other female servants were taken to Little Rock to cook for the troops.

She did her duty, but the young woman could scarcely keep from being somewhat dazzled by traveling around the South seeing new places. She performed different functions within the unit, and she got a first-hand look at military life. She was sent to Washington, D.C. to be a cook and laundress for a general and his staff.

Miss Williams was on the front lines with the troops as they raided the Shenandoah Valley, then they went to St. Louis for a while. Congress passed an act authorizing the establishment of the first all African-American units of the military. These units would become known as "Buffalo Soldiers".

Miss Williams finally joined the Army intending to provide a living for herself. Fiercely independent, she did not want to depend on others. She enlisted in the autumn of 1866 in the 38th United States

Infantry calling herself William Cathay. Buffalo Soldiers, who served from Montana to Texas, would play a major role in the history of the West. They would build forts and roads, protect railroad crews, escort trains and stages and help fight hostile Native Americans.

Private Cathay learned how to use a musket and how to perform guard duty. The excitement started when the unit was deployed to protect immigrants traveling to one of the then most dangerous routes to California. It was an exciting time, but it was a hard life in spite of the steady paycheck.

Private Cathay was growing tired of the rigors of Army life after two years of service. She said she was ill and doctors examined her; they discovered she was a woman. She was honorably discharged in October 1868. Her place in history as the first female Buffalo Soldier was ensured.

Madewood Plantation
Napoleonville, Louisiana

Madewood Plantation

Mr. Thomas Pugh left North Carolina to seek his fortune in Louisiana. He settled in the rich agricultural section of Bayou Lafourche and amassed enormous wealth as a sugar cane planter.

It took him and his wife Eliza eight years to have their dream house, Madewood Plantation, constructed. Designed by well-known architect Henry Howard, the elegant twenty-one room Greek Revival mansion was built in 1846. Its unusual name was derived from the fact that it was constructed of wood from trees on the expansive property.

Sadly, Mr. Pugh died of yellow fever in 1852. He was unable to enjoy the beautiful home for long. Miss Pugh carried on at Madewood until her death in 1885.

A classic example of an antebellum mansion, Madewood is one of the larger Louisiana plantation houses. It was bought and lovingly restored in 1964 by Miss Naomi and Mr. Harold Marshall. In 1983, Madewood Plantation was designated a National Historic Landmark.

The house has been in motion pictures, and it has been featured in several publications. It now offers tours and graciously hosts overnight guests.

Vivandieres or
"Daughters of the Regiment"

There was a small group of patriotic women known as vivandieres that served both Armies in a quasi-military capacity. Often the daughter or the wife of an officer, they were also called "Daughters of the Regiment". They first appeared in French armies during the Napoleanic period, and their presence in the American Civil War was helpful and appreciated.

Vivandieres wore clever, colorful costumes of a short, full skirt that covered trousers and a short jacket. Their duties were to provide immediate triage-type assistance for the wounded both on and off the battlefield. They also carried colors, marched with their unit, wrote letters for soldiers, cooked and most important of all, offered moral support. Many were armed for self-defense.

As the War dragged on and campaigns covered longer distances, vivandieres appeared less often. In the autumn of 1864 within months of the War's end, General Grant ordered that all women be removed from military camps in his theater.

The stories of some well-known Daughters of the Regiment follow, and it soon becomes apparent that their dedicated

service to their country sometimes took on
dangerous and daring aspects.

Kady Brownell

Miss Kady Brownell was an enlisted man's wife who resolutely followed her husband Robert onto the battlefield. She had no idea what fate awaited her, and she became a newspaper's darling.

She saw fighting at the Battles of Bull Run and at the Battle of New Bern, North Carolina. She was allowed to carry a flag at the First Bull Run. Reportedly, she received a wound during that battle for which she requested a pension. A pension was later awarded by a special act of Congress -- not for her wound but for her good works during the War.

She was officially a laundress with the 5th Rhode Island Battalion. She offered to carry the colors into the Battle of New Bern. After the 5th Battalion reached the battle line, she was ordered to the rear to tend to the wounded, where there was a greater need. She kept the 5th from firing on a gray overcoated Union unit appearing at the 5th's rear. She accomplished this vital mission by waving a flag as she ran back and forth.

In April 1862, she and her husband went to New York. She was both delighted and surprised when newspapers there glowingly hailed her as "The Heroine of New Bern". The flag she carried at New

Bern was returned to her after the War. One can be sure it occupied a place of honor in her home!

Bridget Divers

Miss Bridget Divers was actually a cross between a vivandiere and a soldier. She was born in Ireland and emigrated to America. When in her early twenties, she joined her husband in the First Michigan Cavalry unwilling to be separated from him. She was soon known affectionately by the troops as "Irish Biddy" and "Michigan Bridget".

She tended to the wounded, and she mothered soldiers in the unit. She also kept up the morale of her unit. She wrote letters home for men who could not, and she lent a comforting and sympathetic ear when they told her their fears and troubles. She also helped out around camp wherever she was needed. In those ways, she performed the duties associated with vivandieres.

However, she was also fearless, and she became a substitute soldier when riding side by side with her husband. If a man fell, she quickly took his place. She reportedly had two horses shot out from under her in the heat of battle -- a little too close for comfort! It is no wonder she was well respected by the First Michigan Cavalry.

As well known as she was during the War Between the States, the story ends there. Not much is known of her after the

War ended. She remained with the Army and rode west with a detachment to advance and defend the rough and ready frontier. No doubt she enjoyed the raw excitement of helping to tame the Wild West.

Annie Etheridge

She was born Miss Lorinda Anna Blair in Detroit to a privileged background, but the family lost its fortune when she was twelve. Poverty became the order of the day. In 1860 when she was around twenty years of age, she married Mr. James Etheridge.

She followed her husband into war; he deserted quickly, but she decided to stay. She served as a "Daughter of the Regiment" to the 3rd Michigan for three years, then she went to the 5th Michigan where she served for four years.

Miss Etheridge saw many fierce, bloody battles -- both Bull Runs, Antietam, Gettysburg, Fredericksburg, Chancellorsville, Spotsylvania. She acted as a field nurse, and she spent time both in an army hospital and on board a hospital transport ship.

Reserved and plainly dressed, she carried pistols. "Gentle Annie" cooked a bit in camp and generally did whatever else needed to be done. Often finding herself in the thick of battle, she was fearless. She was awarded The Kearney Cross (for non-commissioned officers and privates) for her bravery.

She wanted to write a book at war's end but never got around to it. She got a job as a clerk in the United States

Pension Office. Having jettisoned her war deserter husband, she married veteran Mr. Charles Hooks in 1870. In 1886, she was awarded a twenty-five dollar a month pension for her wartime service.

Miss Etheridge was awarded an exceptional honor in 1913 when she was buried in Arlington National Cemetery.

Major Belle Reynolds

Miss Arabella "Belle" Reynolds, born in 1843, was a Daughter of the Regiment who followed her enlisted husband into war as part of the 17th Illinois Infantry. She did not engage in any military or paramilitary efforts but nevertheless rose to the rank of major. She performed the duties of nurse and other camp duties.

Born in Massachusetts, she and her family went to unsettled Iowa when she was fourteen years old. She later became an Iowa schoolteacher. She married Mr. John Reynolds in 1860, and they moved to Peoria, Illinois.

When her husband enlisted, she stayed with him despite the disapproval of the regiment's colonel. She was tall and kindly, and the soldiers liked her very much. She tended to their medical needs, sewed for them and solicited public support for people to make the soldiers' lives easier.

She traveled with the regiment by way of army wagon, ambulance or mule. Sometimes, carrying a musket, she walked proudly with the unit. She saw a number of battles: Forts Henry and Donelson, Shiloh, Vicksburg. She stayed with the 17th until the fall of 1864.

She sewed on board the hospital ship The Emerald; the ship was docked near Shiloh to transport the most seriously

injured Yankees to the North.   All of a
sudden, there was a terrible commotion as
Northern soldiers began to storm the ship
in order to escape the fighting. Miss
Reynolds found herself having to prevent
them from coming aboard.   She grimly
confronted them with a pistol an army
captain gave her for that purpose.
Thankfully, fresh troops arrived, allowing
her to tend to injured men on board.   She
described the whole scene as one of chaos
and pain.

Just over a week after Shiloh on
April 16, 1862, Illinois Governor Richard
Yates formally recognized her as a
daughter of the regiment and gave her an
honorary commission as a major.   The honor
did not alter her place in the chain of
army command, but it did acknowledge her
value to the Army.

Soon after, Mr. Reynolds' enlistment
expired, and he and his wife left the
Army.   They moved to California.

Nadine Turchin

Miss Nadine Turchin never received the official designation of daughter of the regiment, but her military role was clear. She was raised as Nedezhda Lvova in military camps in Europe as the daughter of a Russian army officer. Her husband John was also Russian. They married in Cracow, Russia in 1856 and emigrated to America. They settled in Illinois where Mr. Turchin worked as an engineer for the railroad.

He was appointed a colonel in command of the 19th Illinois Infantry in mid-1861. His thirty-five-year-old wife followed him into army life. She would be seen as the regiment's mother figure; she acted mainly in a nursing capacity. She also kept the morale of the troops up and performed whatever duties needed to be done around camp.

During a brief illness of her husband's she took his place as regimental commander. She provided leadership to the regiment with no complaints from the troops -- they respected and admired her. Although stories flew that she had led the regiment into battle, it would be very doubtful she would have been permitted to do so. More likely, she kept the regiment running smoothly during her husband's illness.

In the summer of 1862, Colonel Turchin was court martialed partially because of charges that he had violated orders prohibiting military wives in some areas from following their husbands into the field. He was found guilty on that charge. It would have difficult to deny the high profile role his wife took in camp. He was dismissed from the service, but President Lincoln overruled the decision and made him a brigadier general. From that point on, Miss Turchin kept a very low profile, staying in the rear of the regiment. She did not want to do further harm to her husband's military career.

She was bored with army life and found efforts to fill her days lacking purpose and fulfillment. She liked it when the regiment saw combat (or even the possibility of fighting), for that meant excitement and a respite from the tedium of her days. She got as close as possible to the action while keeping a low profile. She kept a diary which gave an insight into the workings of an army regiment. Even though she was a general's wife, she never asked for any favors or special treatment. The Turchins left the service in the fall of 1864. They eventually wound up in Illinois, and they were poor. Mr. Turchin finally received a fifty-dollar-a-month pension in 1900. When he died a year later, his wife applied for a widow's pension of thirty-dollars-a-month. She received it in 1902, and it was her source of financial support until her death in 1904.

Magnolia Plantation and Gardens
Charleston, South Carolina

Coming across the Pond from England in the mid-1600s, wealthy Mr. Thomas Drayton and his namesake went to Barbados. In the late 1600s, a restless Thomas, Jr. made his way to Charleston. That same year, Mr. Stephen Fox also came from Barbados to Charleston. He went to what would be called Magnolia Plantation. Mr. Drayton married his daughter, Ann; the resulting family ownership has extended through three hundred years.

At the first house (1680-1811) during the Revolutionary War, the British camped at Magnolia using its river bluff for their Ashley River encirclement of Charleston. The mansion burned down thirty years later.

The second house (1811-1865) was moved to a nearby site which offered a lovely view of the tranquil Ashley River. This house was burned in 1865 by General Sherman's troops. The owner, Reverend John Grimke Drayton, owned a modest summer house in North Carolina. He had the cottage disassembled and floated to the ruins of Magnolia Plantation. He mounted the cottage on Magnolia's burned-out floor. The house was expanded through the years.

His aunts were the notorious Grimke sisters, Misses Angelina and Sarah. The sisters' opposition to slavery caused their official banishment from South Carolina. They went North and continued their antislavery and women's rights efforts.

Previously in 1820, having no male heirs, Mr. Thomas Drayton, great grandson of Magnolia's first Drayton, willed the estate to his daughter's sons, Messrs. Thomas and John Grimke. The stipulation was that they assume the Drayton name. Thomas died in a hunting accident, and brother John (in England preparing for the ministry) found himself a wealthy plantation owner at the age of twenty-two. He married Miss Julia Ewing.

Enhancing the plantation's gardens became a life-long labor of love for Reverend Drayton. He introduced the first azaleas to America and in 1870, he opened Magnolia's gardens to a grateful public. There are thirty acres of gardens, and it is the oldest major public garden in America.

Magnolia Plantation is listed in the National Register of Historic Places, and it is the oldest plantation on the Ashley River. All told, there are five hundred acres of gardens and grounds to explore, encompassing a Biblical Garden, an Herb Garden, a Camellia Garden, a Barbados Tropical Garden, a Maze, a Topiary Garden, a petting zoo, and a five-hundred acre Wildlife Sanctuary.

The residence itself is open for tours, and the house and gardens welcome between 150,000 and 200,000 visitors a year.

Spies

Perhaps the most romantic-sounding of the famous women in the Civil War were spies. How exciting and dangerous the espionage sounds! Most female spies worked for the Confederacy, but the North had its share.

Aiding the women's efforts was the fact that no honorable male would dare "frisk" a female. Men could search belongings, but personal touching was strongly discouraged, although it no doubt took place. The story is told of a ten-year-old Southern girl who regularly walked to town with her father. There, her pockets would be stuffed with much needed medicines and supplies for Confederate soldiers. Her father would always be searched, but the little girl would go untouched, free to smuggle again.

Intelligence and cunning were necessary traits for spies. No one could doubt that good looks and feminine wiles also played a large part in espionage efforts. Ingenuity and a cool head were also valuable characteristics -- one Confederate spy smuggled messages inside a hollowed-out hambone, while others sewed messages and/or supplies into hems. It took a certain kind of personality to engage in the dangers of spying.

While most spies did what they did mainly to help their country, they no

doubt also enjoyed the excitement and
danger. They would be charged with
treason if caught, and a death sentence
could be the consequence.

Mary Elizabeth Bowser

Miss Mary Elizabeth Bowser was born on a plantation near Richmond as a slave to planter Mr. John Van Lew. After his death in 1851, his slaves were freed. Miss Bowser had been sent by the family to be educated in Philadelphia. She married Mr. Wilson Bowser, a free man.

She continued to work for the Van Lew family as a paid servant. She was especially close to Miss Elizabeth Van Lew, a daughter of the family. The two women hatched an ingenious plan to spy on the Confederacy.

During the War, the attractive Miss Bowser served as a spy for General Ulysses S. Grant. She accomplished this by becoming a servant in President Jefferson Davis' Richmond home, gathering vital military information for General Grant. One could not get closer to the source than to work in the home of the President of the Confederate States of America!

She pretended to be slightly simple-minded or crazy; in this way, she became privy to more intelligence. She listened carefully as President Davis and his cronies ate their meals. People talked more freely around her, figuring she could not comprehend what she heard. By letting down their guard, they sometimes said far too much. Miss Bowser then passed the information on to the waiting Miss Van Lew who wrote it in code.

Miss Bowser recorded the exciting details of her spying efforts in a diary.

Belle Boyd

Miss Maria Isabella "Belle" Boyd was born in Martinsburg, Virginia (later to become West Virginia in 1863 when western counties of Virginia joined the Union) in 1844. She received a fine education at the Mount Washington Female College of Baltimore from the ages of twelve to sixteen. She was extremely pretty, a true Southern belle, and her looks would aid her in her spying.

In July 1861, Federal troops occupied Martinsburg. They barged into the Boyd home and for some reason attempted to raise a Union flag on the roof. Mr. Boyd was not present, and things quickly got out of hand with no male protection for the Boyd females. As the situation escalated, one of the bullies pushed Miss Boyd's mother, so the teenaged Miss Belle shot him (not fatally). She was not found guilty of any felony.

Her father operated a hotel in Front Royal, Virginia some forty miles from the Union capital. Miss Boyd operated from the hotel, eavesdropping on conversations among military men. The men liked having the pretty teenager around, so perhaps they boasted a bit or let their guards down. She was soon racing on horseback to relay valuable information to Generals Turner Ashby and Stonewall Jackson during the spring 1862 Shenandoah Valley campaign.

She started to use a cipher code and was arrested in March 1862. She was held for a week before being released with a warning to stop spying or face more dire consequences. General Stonewall Jackson had made her an honorary captain and aide-de-camp. She was not about to stop trying to help the Confederacy. That would be like asking birds to stop flying!

Back in Front Royal, she continued to gather information from unsuspecting Federal officers. She was arrested again on July 30, 1862 and taken to the Old Capitol Prison in Washington, D.C. She not surprisingly refused to take the Union oath of allegiance and was imprisoned for a month.

She was kept in solitary confinement for most of that time, and her health suffered. Sympathetic Union officers felt a little sorry for her because she was so young and pretty; maybe she would listen to them this time since imprisonment did not seem to agree with her, they thought. She was released and banished to Richmond. Again, she was sternly commanded to cease her spying. They were confident she had seen the error of her ways after her unpleasant prison experience.

She quickly left Richmond and happily toured her beloved South for a few months, coming home to occupied Martinsburg early in 1863. She was arrested a third time that summer because she was in Federal territory in violation of the terms of her banishment. She was jailed at Carroll Prison in Washington, D.C. for three months.

She was released after contracting typhoid and was sent to England to recuperate. Some people say she carried information for the Confederacy to English sympathizers with her.

On her return to America, she faced more excitement. The blockade runner on which she was a passenger was captured after a merry chase. She fell in love with Mr. Samuel Hardinge, an officer on the Union ship. They married in England on August 25, 1864.

Mr. Hardinge had been dropped from the Navy for "neglect of duty". He had allowed the beguiling Miss Boyd to proceed to Canada, then on to England. Their marriage was tragically cut short when he died suddenly soon after the War ended.

Miss Boyd certainly had more than enough war experiences to fill a book, so she wrote her memoir. The book had the intriguing title, <u>Belle Boyd in Camp and Prison</u>. Never one to shun the spotlight, she gladly did the lecture circuit to promote it.

She also began a theatrical career, touring America and England. She played largely on her experiences as a Confederate spy. In the years immediately following the War, people were anxious to hear war stories. Rapt audiences flocked to listen to the beautiful former spy tell of daring escapades.

Excitement was still to be present in her life. She bore three children to two men. The father of her first child was her second husband, Mr. John S. Hammond, a former officer of the British Army. They lived in California and eventually divorced. She then married Mr. Nathaniel

High.

While touring the western states, Miss Boyd died at the age of sixty-seven of a heart attack in 1900.

Major Pauline Cushman

Born in New Orleans in 1833, Miss Pauline Cushman's family moved to Michigan. The attractive woman did an extremely unusual thing for a women of that time -- she ran off at age eighteen to New York City to pursue an acting career! She toured the United States in plays. She would later use her acting abilities and her southern birth to spy for the Union at the start of the War.

She was appearing in a road show in Louisville when two paroled Confederate officers offered her a sizable amount of money to toast President Davis during her performance. That would be a daring thing to do in a border state. She made the toast after reporting the request to the federal provost marshal. He recognized that this feigned expression of Southern loyalty would give her entrée into Confederate camps. The theater company fired her, and she was elevated even higher in the rebels' eyes.

Piteously claiming to be looking for her officer brother, she tugged at the heartstrings of many a Southern camp. She followed the CSA Army and quickly became the darling of unwitting Southern troops. She gathered information that would be invaluable to advancing Union forces.

She was captured in 1863 with

compromising papers and taken to the headquarters of General Braxton Bragg in Tennessee. There, she was sentenced to be hanged in ten days. Before her execution, Union forces captured Shelbyville and set her free.

She continued to spy for the Union, and President Lincoln awarded her an honorary major's commission. She was now too recognizable to spy, so she toured the country in uniform lecturing about her wartime escapades. As with any good performer, the stories were embellished with each performance.

After the War, she made her way to San Francisco where she returned to acting. Mr. Ferdinand Sarmiento wrote an 1865 biography of her entitled, The Life of Pauline Cushman. Racked by a painful illness, she committed suicide in late 1893. She was buried with military honors in the cemetery of the San Francisco Grand Army of the Republic.

Antonia Ford

Miss Antonia Ford was a beautiful Virginia native who grew up with a life of genteel comfort. In 1861, General J.E.B. Stuart named the twenty-three-year-old beauty an honorary member of his staff. In the summer of 1861, Federal troops occupied Fairfax, and they moved into the Ford home.

Miss Ford flirted shamelessly with the handsome soldiers in blue. She gathered vital bits of information which she relayed to General Stuart. At one point, she drove herself twenty miles through rain to deliver a message to him.

In December 1862, Union Brigadier General Edwin Stoughton made his headquarters at the Fairfax Courthouse. His mission was to fortify the nearby Federal capital. Miss Ford monitored the movement of Union soldiers and reported to Generals Stuart and John Mosby.

She took to riding with General Stoughton, and soon gossip floated among his troops. It did not seem appropriate that their commander would be consorting so openly with the enemy. Perhaps he should have been wary of the beautiful Miss Ford.

In March 1863, General Mosby picked up General Stoughton, forty of his soldiers, and horses and weapons while the General and his troops slept. Earlier that evening, there had been a big party and everyone was sleeping it off.

General Mosby vehemently denied that Miss Ford had provided him with information that led to the raid, but General Stoughton was irate. He was convinced his lovely companion was the culprit. A female Union employee was sent to the Ford house posing as a Confederate sympathizer.

The kindly Fords took her in, and she and Miss Ford bonded. They shared stories of Confederate service, and Miss Ford learned to trust her. After a few months, Miss Ford proudly showed off her commission from General Stuart.

She was arrested and taken to the Old Capitol Prison. There, a Union officer, Major Joseph Willard, became infatuated with her. He worked diligently to gain her release. After her release, he proposed and she asked him to resign his U.S. Army commission. He obliged, and they were married in the spring of 1864.

They settled into a lovely, grand house in Washington, D.C. They had three children, two of whom died in infancy. Their surviving child, Joseph, had an illustrious career. After getting his law degree from the University of Virginia, he served as ambassador to Spain under President Woodrow Wilson. He later served as a lieutenant governor of Virginia, and he eventually inherited the renowned Willard Hotel.

Sadly, his mother did not live to see her son's distinguished career; she died in 1871.

Rose O'Neal Greenhow

Most men are easily captivated by beautiful women, especially by tragic young widows. Men of the Civil War era were no exceptions. A stunning socialite who lived in Washington, D.C. repeatedly wheedled sensitive and vital information to help the CSA's cause. Military leaders on both sides believed this living doll was largely responsible for the Union's totally unexpected defeat at the First Bull Run.

The woman was Miss Rose O'Neal Greenhow. She moved in society's elite circles, and she had in her lacy pocket top military officers, politicians and presidents. Born in Port Tobacco, Maryland, her father was killed by a servant when she was a toddler.

She and her sisters eventually found their way to Washington, D.C. where she became famous for her beauty. To add to her allure, she had inherited land and money. In her teens, she and her sisters lived with their aunt in a nice Capitol Hill boardinghouse. Miss O'Neal was tall and striking, and she became known as "The Wild Rose".

Men fell all over themselves around her. Being interested in politics, she often sat in on Senate hearings. She learned how to deal with all sorts of men, from the refined to the coarse. This knowledge would aid her greatly in her later spying efforts.

In 1835, she married Dr. Robert Greenhow, a Virginia lawyer and linguist. They lived in Montgomery County, Maryland about thirty miles from the Nation's Capital. They had four daughters: Florence, Gertrude, Leila and Rose. Dr. Greenhow worked with the State Department and often traveled for it. The Greenhows knew Mr. John C. Calhoun -- he often stayed with them when the Senate was in session. The luxury-loving Miss Greenhow was a vibrant part of Washington, D.C.'s inner circle, and she felt very comfortable in the political city.

In the summer of 1850, the Greenhows lived in exotic Mexico City because of Dr. Greenhow's work with the State Department. His wife jumped immediately into the diplomatic set's balls and banquets, and she charmed everyone with her grace and wit.

That fall, they went to San Francisco where Dr. Greenhow opened a law office to settle land claims. It was an exciting time to be in the West -- just after the Gold Rush. Many 49er's crowded the city trying to make a living.

Miss Greenhow was back east caring for her fourth baby when Dr. Greenhow fell down an embankment in San Francisco. He died six weeks later at the age of fifty-four. His wife was unable to be there because the long trip would have been too strenuous after recently giving birth.

Miss Greenhow soon left the children at home and went west. She sailed through the Caribbean, then took a train, then an adventurous journey. She sued the city of San Francisco for her husband's death and won a nominal amount.

Back at home, she sold the marital house, and Mr. Jefferson Davis helped her find a new place on 16th Street. The house would become espionage headquarters for the CSA.

She promoted Mr. James Buchanan for President and returned to California in the summer of 1862 to campaign for him. She returned home that fall, and gossips had a field day about her and the handsome new President. Now in her forties, she looked stunning at the inaugural ball. It seemed she was always fighting rumors and gossip about herself and gentlemen, but the gossip never seemed to faze her.

Her eldest daughter married, and Miss Greenhow went back to San Francisco. She enjoyed seeing the many wonderful changes taking place in the Wild West town. She would always have a soft spot for the place.

In 1858, she was back home and could feel the political tension between the North and the South. She later wept openly in the Senate gallery when Mississippi seceded and Mr. Davis grimly left the Senate. Tragedy struck when daughter Gertrude died in March 1861 after a long illness. The grieving mother vowed never to again wear anything but black.

Two weeks after Fort Sumter, she became a central figure in an espionage system established by Colonel Thomas Jordan. The beauty easily pumped young military and government men for details about Union affairs. She gleaned details the men did not even realize they had let slip.

In the First Battle of Bull Run, Miss Greenhow was instrumental in delivering three messages that forewarned the South of the North's battle plans. This information enabled General Beauregard to revise his own strategy, thus ensuring a Confederate victory. Miss Greenhow was in New York at the time seeing daughter Leila off for a trip. Another person had delivered the messages at Miss Greenhow's instruction.

Mysterious people now came and went to her house at all hours of the day and night. The spy network was intricate. Washington, D.C.'s jaded society culture welcomed The Wild Rose's public antics like a breath of fresh air.

By August of 1861, suspicious private detectives were trailing her. In late August, Mr. Allen Pinkerton and his detectives arrested her at her house. "Confederate Rose" swallowed a spy note when she realized she was being arrested. The detectives did not find the information she was trying to keep hidden. She slipped the papers to a friend who had shown up to see what was causing the ruckus.

Her home was turned into a jail, and other female spies joined her there. While out walking with her guards one day, the resourceful spy threw a ball of pink yarn to a woman who had just been released. Naturally, a message for the Confederacy was inside. Miss Greenhow wrote coded letters to others, but the game was up when the War Department figured out the code. Undaunted, she simply changed the code and continued doing what she was doing.

In January 1862, the picture changed when she was suddenly moved to the Old Capitol Prison. Little Rose was there with her. The child failed to thrive under the unnatural conditions, and Miss Greenhow herself was constantly ill. She secretly sewed a Confederate flag and proudly waved it from the window.

Her March 1862 trial did not go well. She was ordered to go South and to stop spying. General McClellan did not want "Rebel Rose" released because he knew she would go back to spying. She left prison and arrived in Richmond early in June.

She was immediately back in business as a spy. She received a large check from President Davis for her services; she frequently called on the Davises. She engaged in a mad whirl of dancing, music, teas and picnics for the soldiers. The women all wanted to look beautiful to cheer their military men up. She also sewed and knitted for the cause.

Meanwhile, she was secretly putting her prison diary in order for publication. In August 1863, she went to London to get the book published and to try to rustle up sympathy for the Confederacy. She was presented at court in Paris where she met the Emperor of France. Little Rose was put in school in Paris. Mother and daughter parted ways with Miss Greenhow bound for England.

Her book, <u>My Imprisonment and the First Year of Abolition Rule at Washington</u> was selling well. Her publisher had brought it out right after she left America, and Miss Greenhow became an instant celebrity moving among London's best. To add to her dazzling life, she was engaged to recent widower Lord Granville.

The lovely belle wrote and lectured, but her clandestine efforts did not cease. She conspired with British Commander Maury who was instrumental in the success of the CSA Navy. He was devoted to the Confederacy. Miss Greenhow had found many Confederate sympathizers, and she was determined to take clothes back for Southern women who needed them. She planned to make a trip back to report to President Davis on the shipping situation in order to aid blockade running efforts.

A year after her arrival in England, she made her trip leaving for America for a short visit. She was to marry Lord Granville upon her return to England. She left laden down with gold -- all the proceeds from her book, as well as clothes for Southern women. She also carried vital information for President Davis that she hoped might turn the tide of the War.

She sailed on The Condor, a new blockade runner. She wore a large leather pouch around her neck; no one realized it contained two thousand dollars in gold and hundreds of sovereigns. The ship sailed across the Atlantic without incident.

On September 24, they sailed from Halifax, and the warning was out to catch the sleek Condor. A Union boat, The Niphon, spotted her at North Carolina's Cape Fear River on October 1. The Niphon gave chase in the darkness, and the Confederate captain was unaware of the pursuit.

A horrible, horrible storm was raging in the night, and The Condor finally spotted her enemy. Gunshots rang out above the howling of the wind. The blockade runner was only two hundred feet from Confederate Fort Fisher where safety awaited.

Miss Greenhow knew that she would go back to prison or worse if she were captured. She asked the captain to send her ashore in a small boat. He told her she was safe onboard -- they would get to Fort Fisher and she could go on her way. Unconvinced, she threw a fit, and the captain reluctantly gave in to her demands.

Clutching her money bag, she climbed into a boat with a pilot and two other men. The boat bobbed and lurched in the roiling river, but it seemed they were getting closer to shore. Miss Greenhow was certain President Davis would get the dispatches she carried, and she was also sure her gold would find its way into a bank. Then just as it looked as if all would be fine, a huge wave washed over the boat, capsizing it!

Miss Greenhow sank at once, the fortune in gold weighing her down. The men tried to find her, but their efforts were in vain -- she had disappeared in the churning, inky water. She died for the Confederacy just as she had said she would. The others in the boat were saved. A search was immediately launched for her body, but someone else found it first.

A soldier found her body, took all the gold, dragged her to the river's edge and pushed her back in. Her body soon washed ashore again. When the thief learned of her identify as a devoted supporter of the Confederacy, he was contrite and quickly returned the money. The dispatches she carried for President Davis were lost forever. No one would ever know what effect they might have had on the Confederacy's future.

An honor guard was in attendance as Miss Greenhow laid regally in state. She was buried with full military honors, her coffin draped with a Confederate flag. She would have been proud.

Nancy Hart

Miss Nancy Hart was a cute young woman who played the part of innocent country girl to advantage for the Confederate cause. Born in 1846 in North Carolina, she grew up in Virginia. She was a "dead eye" shot with a rifle, and she was an expert horsewoman.

In the autumn of 1861, she was to move in with her sister and brother-in-law, the William Prices. On that day, Union soldiers galloped into the yard and informed Mr. Price that he had to make a speech in town that night favoring the Union. He never got to town -- he was found three days later shot in the back. If Miss Hart had hated Union soldiers before the murder, her loathing now grew deeper.

At a neighbor's party soon after Mr. Price's death, Union soldiers rode past the house in the dark. The party music stopped and Miss Hart shouted, "Hurrah for Jeff Davis". Four shots rang out, one lodging within a hair's breath of her.

Three nights later, she rode off to do her bit for the CSA. She joined the Moccasin Rangers, pro-Southern guerillas, for a time. She served as a scout, guide and spy, carrying messages under a blanket of darkness. She sold eggs and produce to Yankees in order to spy on them. Few soldiers could resist the pretty teenager, so they hung around and she gathered information.

She knew where the isolated mountain outposts were, and she was able to report their manpower and vulnerability to General Jackson. She led his cavalry on raids against the Union.

By the summer of 1862, a large reward was offered for her capture by Lt. Colonel Starr. She was captured at a log cabin and jailed in an old house. She did not take kindly to being incarcerated, so she made friends with one of her guards who was smitten with her. She shot him dead after getting his weapon away from him. She dove out the window, hopped on Lt. Colonel Starr's horse and rode as if her life depended on it -- which it probably did.

A week later, still riding Starr's horse, she returned at night to the scene of her incarceration. With her were two hundred of Virginia's finest soldiers. They raided the town, set fire to a couple of houses, and took many mules, horses and prisoners (including Starr).

Miss Hart soon found herself nursing a young man, Mr. Joshua Davis, back to health. He had been dying from his battle wounds. After the War ended, he came back to the area and married Miss Hart. They had two sons, and the family lived a peaceful life in North Carolina.

The Moon Sisters

The Moon sisters were, by all accounts, quite a handful. They certainly gave the Union Army a run for its money. Miss Lottie and her younger sister Ginnie were born in Virginia, daughters of a doctor. They moved to Ohio as children, but their strong southern ties would never be broken.

The pretty sisters had their choice of many beaus. Miss Lottie was courted ardently by Mr. Ambrose Burnside who would later became a famous Union general in the War Between the States. He would much later come to hold her future in his hands.

Miss Ginnie left the Oxford Female College in the 1860s and went to live with the Clark family. She married Mr. Jim Clark who later became a judge. He was active in the Knights of the Golden Circle -- a Confederate underground organization. Since the Moon sisters were pro-Confederate, Mr. Clark's sympathies in that regard were fortunate.

A courier arrived at the Clark house one day with a secret message that had to be carried to General Kirby Smith in Kentucky. Miss Ginnie Clark volunteered to deliver it and thereby began her dangerous life as a spy. Casting about in her mind for a way to accomplish the mission, she got an idea. She disguised herself as an old woman and headed for Lexington by boat. The mission was accomplished, and she returned by train.

She carried many more messages for the South. She made her way to Washington, D.C. with forged papers that made her a British subject. She talked wary Union officials into letting her go to Virginia "for her health". Once across enemy lines, she delivered messages and went home to her worried husband.

Meanwhile, sister Lottie and their mother, Miss Cynthia Moon, were in Memphis nursing wounded rebel soldiers. Trouble brewed as Union troops ominously drew closer. Nursing was certainly worthwhile, vital work, but Miss Lottie began to wonder if she could contribute even more to the cause. Inspired by sister Ginnie's spying efforts, she made a decision.

She began passing through Yankee lines by pretending to meet a beau. No doubt good looks and innate Southern wiles helped get her past Union soldiers. By using this ruse, she carried information and supplies. She and her mother made more dangerous trips. By this time, the Union had figured out they were Confederate spies. The Federals were biding their time like big old spiders; they would pounce when the time was right.

On the way to Mississippi from Ohio, Miss Lottie and her mother thought they had completed another successful mission. To their surprise, a Union captain entered their boat cabin and brashly prepared to search them. Apparently, he did not know or care that he should not attempt to do such a thing. He persisted in his foolish insistence on searching the women; that would prove to be a mistake.

Suddenly, Miss Lottie pulled out her small, trusty Colt revolver and waved it at him. That was the last thing the captain expected to see! Waving the gun at him, she said that she was a friend of General Burnside and the captain should behave himself. She demanded to see General Burnside. The captain backed down. Miss Lottie swallowed the most important of the dispatches she carried when he left her alone for a few minutes.

She and her mother were put under house arrest at a hotel. Miss Lottie and General Burnside met the next day. She asked her former beau to release them; he refused. No action was ever taken, however, and the charges were dropped. Perhaps he still harbored tender feelings for her. Her sister was ordered to report to Union soldiers daily. Apparently she was still doing things to arouse the suspicions of the Yankees. She was finally ordered to stay out of the Union area.

Miss Ginnie Clark went to Memphis after the War. Miss Lottie became a journalist and got to write about all sorts of interesting things. Not much is known of her life after that time.

Miss Ginnie tried to settle down and be a good housewife, but she apparently grew restless after the excitement of being a spy. She ambled around the country for a while exposing herself to new places and different people. Amazingly, she wound up in Hollywood where she was once again the center of attention. She had bit parts in a couple of 1920s pictures -- <u>The Spanish Dancers</u> and <u>Robin Hood</u>. After that adventure, she moved to Greenwich Village. There, she held court as a grande dame until her death at the age of eighty-one.

Sarah E. Thompson

Miss Sarah Lane was born in Tennessee in 1838. She married Mr. Sylvanius Thompson in 1854, and they had two children. Mr. Thompson joined the Union Army and worked mainly as a recruiter. His wife worked with him, assembling and organizing Union sympathizers in Tennessee.

Early in 1864, he was ambushed and killed by a Confederate soldier. Angered by her husband's death, Miss Thompson became a Union spy. She delivered dispatches and relayed information to Union officers.

She reported that CSA Army General John Hunt Morgan and his men were spending the night in Greeneville. Union troops ferreted his camp out, and Miss Thompson reportedly pointed out the General as he desperately hid behind a fence. He was killed.

After that ghastly event, Miss Thompson became an Army nurse in Tennessee and in Cleveland. Having two children to support, she also gave lectures in northern cities about her war experiences. Like many single mothers, she tried to earn money any way she could.

In 1866, she married a New York man, Mr. Orville Bacon, and they had two children. She and Mr. Bacon divorced, and she married Mr. James Cotton in the 1880s. Soon a widow, she struggled to support her family. She worked through many temporary government jobs in Washington, D.C. She was finally awarded a monthly pension of twelve dollars a month in 1897.

On April 21, 1909 in Washington, she died after being struck by an "electric car". She was buried in Arlington National Cemetery.

Elizabeth Van Lew

Virginia belle Miss Elizabeth Van Lew was born in 1818 to a prosperous family. She was sent to Philadelphia to be educated. When she returned to Richmond, she harbored strong anti-slavery feelings. Fueled by her beliefs, she became a Union operative.

Her family's elegant Richmond home became a gathering place for Richmond's elite. Military officers and politicians unwittingly revealed information which Miss Van Lew quickly forwarded to the Union. No one even remotely suspected her of being a spy, and she became ingenious in her ways of gathering information.

She visited Libby Prison which housed Union prisoners of war. She brought baskets of food, medicine and books to the grateful prisoners. The guards, charmed by her and her humanitarian gestures toward the enemy, passed along information to her. She managed to help some prisoners escape, and she also gleaned valuable information from newly captured men. These men eagerly recounted details about the strength and disposition of Confederate troops they had seen on their way to the prison.

She took to dressing quite strangely, and she adopted a guise of being mentally unbalanced. People got used to seeing the spinster they dubbed "Crazy Bet" talk to herself in public. No one would have thought she had the mental ability to be a spy. Consequently, rebel soldiers around town dropped their guard around her.

She got entry into President Davis' home by persuading a former slave, Miss Mary Elizabeth Bowser, to secure a post in the Davis home. Miss Bowser now worked for the Van Lew family as a paid servant. Miss Bowser relayed information to her friend, who developed a cipher code to pass it along.

The Van Lew family had freed their slaves, but many chose to continue to work for them in paid positions. Miss Van Lew sent former slaves northward carrying baskets of produce or flowers. Military people never thought to search the baskets. Mixed in with the eggs or other produce were messages that were relayed to General Grant by an intricate courier system.

At War's end, President Grant rewarded Miss Van Lew's invaluable wartime service with the job of postmistress of Richmond. That she chose to remain in Richmond is amazing, because she was ostracized and vilified by her fellow Southerners. The abuse grew worse as the years passed, and Miss Van Lew could not seem to understand why people were angry with her.

After the postmistress position ended, she lived on an annuity from a Union soldier's family -- she had helped the young man during his incarceration at Libby Prison. She died in Richmond.

Longwood
Natchez, Louisiana

Longwood, the "Oriental Villa", was going to be an architectural masterpiece the likes of which the world had never seen. It would elegantly house cotton nabob Mr. Haller Nutt, his wife Julia and their eight children. Philadelphia architect Mr. Samuel Sloan designed the octagonal palace in 1859, and construction began in 1860.

The mansion would have thirty-two rooms, each with its own entrance onto a balcony, a solarium and an observatory. A Byzantine-Moorish dome with a twenty-four foot finial would reach toward the sky.

Mr. Nutt grew excited as the shell of his house quickly went up. Soon, he would be the envy of everyone with his showplace. Then, the War Between the States began. The Northern craftsmen went home to fight, never to return. A dejected Mr. Nutt, along with some local workers and a few slaves, completed the basement level.

The Nutt family lived in nine basement rooms as the War dragged on. On June 15, 1864, Mr. Nutt died in the house. Miss Nutt and the children continued to live there.

Grandchildren owned Longwood until 1968. It is now maintained and operated for tours by the Pilgrimage Garden Club. The unique house has been named a National Historic Landmark, a Mississippi landmark and an historic site on the Civil War Discovery Trail.

Medics

One female doctor, Dr. Mary Walker, practiced during the Civil War. Scores of brave, compassionate women on both sides were nurses, many of them acting in a volunteer capacity. Most nurses worked tirelessly in crowded military hospitals where they saw myriad gruesome and tragic sights. Others were field nurses working under unimaginably harsh and brutal conditions. The large majority of these women remain unsung heroes -- few records remain of their names.

Miss Dorothea Dix actively recruited women to serve as nurses in the Army Medical Bureau of the United States Army. She wanted recruits to be intelligent and dedicated, but they were also to be plain and middle-aged from the ages of thirty to fifty. Young, fetching women would not be found in abundance in the ranks of nurses.

Civil War nurses were by no means mere supporting players. They were in the trenches, so to speak. They provided critical triage-type assistance, calmed frantic soldiers who were staring into the face of death or amputation, dispensed vital medications, and often saved lives while equally thinly-stretched physicians were engaged with other patients.

Civil War nurses lent sympathetic ears to lonely, wounded young men. Various diseases killed twice as many men as did battle wounds. Nurses rejoiced when a man recovered from a disease, and they were sorry when the outcome was not favorable.

It is no wonder that Civil War nurses were known as "Angels of the Battlefield".

Clara Barton

Miss Clarissa Harlowe Barton was born on Christmas Day, 1821 in Massachusetts. A very bashful child, she called herself Clara from childhood. Her father was a farmer and a leader in local politics. He was a former soldier whose tales of service spurred a lifelong interest in military tactics and strategy in his youngest child.

From the ages of eight to thirteen, Miss Barton was largely confined to the house as she nursed her ill older brother. She found that she liked nursing. She started to do a bit of local nursing while completing her schooling.

At the age of eighteen, she was teaching school in town, then she set up a school in a mill to teach children of factory workers. She went back to college for a while when she was twenty-nine. She then opened a public school in New Jersey.

A dissatisfied, somewhat melancholy frame of mind plagued her for most of her life. To the world, though, she generally projected a bright outlook. After having been ill in 1854, she went to Washington, D.C. seeking a warmer climate. She went to work at the United States Patent Office at a time when most women did not work. Many of her male co-workers criticized and snubbed her.

She was close to forty years old when the War started. She wrote letters for soldiers and delivered medical supplies. Churches in the Northeast were advised of the needs for soldiers; churches, sewing circles and relief organizations responded well. She rented a warehouse and started a distribution agency. She soon became known as the "Angel of the Battlefield".

Miss Barton was most often close to the front where the fighting took place. She saw many, many ghastly sights. Usually wearing stripped print dresses and a kerchief, she assisted at operations in hospitals, tents, farmhouses, barns and out in the open.

Moved by the heartbreak of families, she was instrumental in trying to locate missing soldiers. There were also unknown buried soldiers to hopefully be identified in order to give families closure. Miss Barton had rolls of missing men printed up by the Government Printing Office. Names were arranged by state, and regional newspapers published them. The process of identification went on for years. She was responsible for more than twenty thousand soldiers being identified.

In 1866, Congress paid her fifteen thousand dollars for her wartime service and for her ongoing efforts. From 1866-68, she was a well-known lecturer. The Angel of the Battlefield was becoming a national heroine as she traveled through the Midwest and the Northeast.

She began a long association with the suffrage movement after meeting Miss Susan B. Anthony and Miss Julia Ward Howe. She was behind them in principle but was not an active participant in the movement. By the winter of 1868-69, she had a physical and emotional collapse brought on by doing too much. She kept a very low profile for the next ten years.

She was shrewd with a dollar and had saved a bit. At age forty-eight, she and sister Sally set off for Scotland in the summer of 1869. Her sister went home, but Miss Barton went on to London, then on to Geneva. She went to Rome and then on to Corsica where she found the climate immensely agreeable for her fragile physical health.

She went to Berne and worked as a nurse during the Franco-Prussian War. She became more interested in the Red Cross while in Europe. After four years, she returned to America.

At this point in time, she was ill emotionally and spent a brief period in a New York sanitarium, "Our Home on the Hillside". She found insight into herself and her philosophy of living changed. She was now happy to rest, and she no longer felt compelled to work herself to the point of exhaustion. The sanitarium was in Danville, and she grew fond of the area. The first American Red Cross chapter would be founded there.

In the winter of 1877, nearing sixty, she was ready to make the American Red Cross a household word. She went to Washington, D.C. to generate political interest in the organization's formation. The purpose of the organization would be to offer Americans relief in time of floods, hurricanes, tornadoes, drought and forest fires. The government finally approved the creation of the organization.

The first disaster relief effort for

the American Red Cross was a 1881 forest fire, but Miss Barton was not at the scene. In 1884, she <u>was</u> at the scene after a major flood from the Ohio River happened in Cincinnati. She left that scene for another of tornado devastation in Indiana. She was at the infamous Johnstown flood of 1889 in which three to four thousand people perished.

In 1893, a hurricane claimed one thousand lives as it swept over sea islands, and Miss Barton was there. At the end of 1897, she moved to Glen Echo, Maryland a lovely suburb of Washington, D.C. Her house became the headquarters of the American Red Cross.

In February 1898, she left for Cuba to discuss relief operations for Cuban reconcentrados -- folks who had been herded into concentration camps. She gave out food and medical supplies and worked at hospitals. She returned to Florida aiming to return home, but then the Spanish-American War started. She went right back to Cuba.

Near the age of seventy-nine, she went to Galveston in September 1900 to bring Red Cross relief. The big hurricane and its resulting storm surge had hit, killing six thousand people. Three thousand homes were destroyed; devastation was everywhere. She was there for two months and in Houston where many victims had fled.

At age eighty, she spent the summer of 1902 traveling to Europe to the Seventh International Red Cross Conference in St. Petersburg, Russia. She met the Czar and visited the Summer Garden and the Winter Palace. She found there was much Red

Cross work being done in Russia.

Later in 1902, she sat by President Theodore Roosevelt at the Spanish-American War Veterans Conference. That night, she was the only woman seated at the table of honor at the banquet given for the President.

Miss Barton retired from the American Red Cross in 1904. She died in 1912 at the advanced age of ninety-one.

Dorothea Dix

Miss Dorothea Dix was best known for her extensive work with the mentally ill. She also held a vital position in the Civil War. She was an intelligent, determined woman whose purpose in life seemed to be helping those less fortunate than herself.

She was born in 1802 in Maine to an alcoholic itinerant preacher and his mentally unsound wife. Miss Dix became a child mother to her two younger brothers; she very likely became a parent to her parents as well. She never really got a chance to have much of a childhood. Her paternal grandmother finally took the children in when Miss Dix was twelve.

Miss Dix went to live with her aunt in Worchester, Massachusetts two years later. At a party, she met her second cousin, Mr. Edward Bangs, a successful attorney fourteen years her senior. She told him that she wanted to teach. He suggested she start a "dame school" since girls at that time could not attend public school. They could, however, be taught privately by a woman.

In 1816 at the age of fifteen, Miss Dix became a schoolteacher. She taught her first class of girls aged six to eight. She ran the school successfully for three years.

When she was eighteen, Mr. Bangs totally surprised her by confessing that he had fallen madly in love with her. She closed the school and fled back to her grandmother. Her ardent suitor pursued her and proposed. She accepted but would not set a date. Perhaps her hesitation to marry was fueled by memories of her sketchy upbringing at the hands of her abusive parents.

She told her grandmother that she wanted to open a school for poor girls. The older woman was all in favor of it. Miss Dix's father died at that time, and she returned the engagement ring to a brokenhearted Mr. Bangs.

During the period of 1822-36, she taught classes and began to write children's books. In 1830, she became quite ill. Her friend Dr. Channing asked her to come to St. Croix to tutor his children. The balmy tropical climate did wonders for her, and she returned home invigorated in 1831 at the age of twenty-nine.

In 1836 while caring for her ill grandmother and teaching, she became ill with the then little known disease of tuberculosis. She took an extended vacation to England until the beginning of 1841.

When she was thirty-nine, she volunteered to teach Sunday school for women inmates, some of whom were mentally ill. She was appalled at conditions at the jail. She went to court to better the conditions of the mentally ill. She then visited other jails and almshouses where the mentally ill were poorly housed.

She went all over Massachusetts and

found similar conditions in many places. She eventually delivered a document to the Massachusetts legislature. She was good friends with the governor, and the secretary of state was her former fiancé, Mr. Edward Bangs. Her legislation was favorably received, and funds were made available to expand and improve Worcester State Hospital.

She traveled to other states, covering every state east of the Mississippi. She played a major role in founding thirty-two mental hospitals and many schools for the feeble-minded. She also helped to establish libraries in prisons and in mental hospitals.

After all of this, she went to Europe with the sole intention of resting. Her restful period did not last long at all. She soon found herself inspecting jails and almshouses there as well. She did this work for two years, and she found wretched conditions all over Europe.

At the start of the War, she became the Superintendent of Union Nurses. She was fifty-nine years old, and she was in charge of all women nurses working in Federal army hospitals. She would be kept quite busy in this challenging position.

She sought plain-looking women over the age of thirty, most of whom would not be looking to marry. Miss Dix felt that if nurses were flirting with patients, the patients were possibly being short-changed medically. "Dragon Dix" did not get on particularly well with the military bureaucracy. There were many scraps and tussles with the bureaucracy, but Miss Dix held her own. She usually got what she wanted.

At War's end, she returned to working with the mentally ill. Still in poor health, she spent her last years in a hospital. The champion of the helpless mentally ill died on July 17, 1887.

Phoebe Yates Levy Pember

Miss Phoebe Yates Levy Pember was born in 1823 in Charleston, South Carolina. She was the well-educated daughter of a wealthy Jewish family. In July 1861, she lost her Bostonian husband to tuberculosis.

Miss Pember wanted to help the Confederate cause, and her friend -- the wife of Secretary of State George W. Randolph -- helped her obtain an appointment. Late in December 1862, Miss Pember became the chief matron of the second division of the huge Chimborazo Hospital in Richmond. By War's end, a total of seventy-six thousand patients would have been admitted.

The hospital had several shortages of supplies and medicine, and this was a continual problem for Miss Pember. She also had problems with doctors who did not approve of women's roles in hospitals. She saw many horrors in the hospital, and her goal was to care for sick and wounded soldiers. She ably assisted surgeons in grisly surgeries, and she acted as a companion to the dying. She administered medications and cleaned and dressed wounds.

She remained with the hospital after Richmond fell until the facility was taken over by Federal authorities. In 1879, her exceptional memoirs, <u>A Southern Woman's Story</u>, that unflinchingly told of her hospital days was published. It is an extraordinary piece of work.

The first chapter, <u>Entry Into Man's Domain</u>, told of how men viewed nurses as mere stewards who received minimal pay. Miss Pember wrote that as she came to Chimborazo Hospital initially, doctors visually inspected her. They made no secret of their disdain for women in medicine.

In the second chapter, Miss Pember described her first days at the hospital. She was aghast when shown the small inadequate stove from which meals for hundreds of men would be prepared. She thought of making chicken soup and cut up a raw bird for the first time in her life. She soon learned her way around the small kitchen, becoming a wizard at planning meals using often sparse resources.

In the fourth chapter, <u>Are You Married?</u>, she wrote of inevitable attractions between doctors and nurses. She also spoke of the depreciated Confederate currency and poor pay. She was frustrated because there often was not enough good food to go around.

She told how she wrote a chatty letter for an illiterate soldier confined to his bed. First, she convinced him to cut his long, shaggy hair. He was astonished when she showed him the four-page letter, surprised he had that much to tell his mother. He hoarsely inquired, "Are you married?". She replied that she was a widow. He gently touched her arm and said, "You wait!". For what she was waiting, the refined Miss Pember would never discover!

Another admirer, an uncut diamond convalescing Texan told her that she was "as pretty as a pair of red shoes with green strings". Miss Pember found that comment strangely flattering.

In the sixth chapter, What Comfort Could I Give?, she fretted about the fact that after the April 1863 attack on Drewry's Bluff, the hospital was unprepared to receive the wounded. Vehicles of all types filled with wounded men were rapidly pulling up to the hospital. Miss Pember had received no orders to care for the wounded -- most doctors had departed for the nearby battle site.

She did not want to see men in pain driven around the city to find other hospitals. She got the surgeon in charge to reluctantly allow her to bring the men in. They would be put on the floor, and she would dress wounds. Through the long night, she bathed fractured limbs and dressed wounds.

Her heart broke with sadness when one grievously wounded fellow came through. The doctor told her the situation was hopeless; the soldier should be made as comfortable as possible. On the sixth morning, he looked at her and she lamented silently asking what comfort could she give? He told her that he was the only son of a widow. He asked Miss Pember to tell his mother he died defending his beliefs.

She wrote graphically about incidents of hospital life, and her descriptions of soldiers and events are compelling. She wrote about the collapse of the

Confederacy. She spoke of how different hospital departments began to pack up, anticipating the fall. She told how on April 2, 1865, President Davis was handed a telegram at church. He read it, then calmly left the building. The pastor informed the congregation that the city would soon be evacuated. Everyone was to go home and prepare for it.

Miss Pember vividly described the actions of people as they left the city. She detailed a scene of intense confusion at the railroad station. She told about how warehouses and factories were set on fire by Union troops and that soon Main Street was all ablaze.

In the eighteenth chapter, _A Woman Must Soar Beyond the Conventional_, she told of how she cajoled and bullied Union soldiers after the fall in order to obtain food and other provisions. She was gutsy and rarely came away empty-handed. She tended to her patients even after they were moved to another hospital.

When her nursing duties finally ceased, she was faced with the question of what she would now do. She had a box full of worthless money. The kind people of Virginia saw that she received food daily, and she sometimes had no idea who had delivered it.

Her memoir is a fascinating read which gives a compelling look at war. It also gives clear insight into the challenges faced by women who served as nurses.

Susie King Taylor

Miss Susie King Taylor was born in 1848 about thirty-five miles from Savannah. She became a domestic servant for the Grest Farm. In 1854, her owner permitted her and her brother to live with their grandmother, Miss Dolly Reed, in Savannah. Miss Reed had been freed by Mr. Grest.

There, the youngsters learned to read and write. They had to hide their books because people could get into trouble by teaching African-Americans literacy. The children attended a secret school run by a free woman. Miss Taylor was later taught by friends of the family.

At age fourteen, she saw Union troops around during the War. She was sent to St. Simon's Island, and there she ran a school behind Union lines for around forty African-American children. The school was called Gaston Bluff, and liberated slaves were also students.

She left the island with Union Captain C.T. Trowbridge who had come to the island to recruit African-American troops for the First South Carolina Volunteers, the 33rd Regiment. She went initially as a laundress, then she did some clerical work and nursing. She nursed troops as they traveled and fought in South Carolina, Georgia and Florida.

She had met her husband, Mr. Edward
Taylor on St. Simon's Island. He was a
sergeant in the 33rd Regiment. After the
War, the Taylors settled in Savannah.
Miss Taylor moved to Boston after her
husband's death, and she eventually remarried. The former Civil War nurse died
in 1912.

Captain Sally Tompkins

Miss Sally Louisa Tompkins was born in 1833 to a wealthy coastal Virginia family. She was a lifelong philanthropist who spent a lot of her fortune helping others.

After the First Battle of Bull Run in 1861, she opened her Richmond home to wounded Confederate soldiers as the CSA requested. She implored a friend, Judge Robertson of the Circuit Court of Richmond, to open his as well. At her own expense, Miss Tompkins transformed his house into a hospital, naming it in his honor. Robertson Hospital became one of the most vital institutions in the South. It received the most desperate cases.

Wounded Rebels called Miss Tompkins "the little lady with the milk-white hands". She received dozens of marriage proposals, but she never married. A few weeks after the hospital opened, President Davis placed all Southern hospitals under the control of the Confederate Medical Department. He commissioned Miss Tompkins a captain on September 9, 1861, and her patients began to call her "Captain Sally".

After four war years, Robertson Hospital had admitted one thousand, three hundred and thirty-three patients. Its survival rate was an impressive 94.5 percent, a performance unmatched by any other hospital, North or South.

After exhausting most of her money because of philanthropic efforts, she entered Richmond's Home for Confederate Women in her later years. In 1916, she was buried with full military honors. She was further honored years later when two chapters of the United Daughters of the Confederacy were named for her.

Dr. Mary Walker

Dr. Mary Walker was born on November 26, 1832 on a farm near Oswego, New York. Her forward-thinking carpenter father had built the first schoolhouse for Oswego at his own expense. Her parents, Alvah and Vesta, were abolitionists. Miss Walker first dreamed of becoming a physician while reading some of her father's medical pamphlets.

At age eighteen, she attended Falley Seminary for two terms beginning in December 1850. At age nineteen, she started to teach school in a nearby village; she taught for a couple of years, saving as much as she could.

Doctors were scarce, and she was admitted to Syracuse Medical College in December 1853 at the age of twenty-one. Her schooling would consist of three terms of thirteen weeks each. In between terms, students worked with a practicing physician. She received instruction in anatomy, surgery, medical practice, pathology, obstetrics, diseases of women and children, physiology, pharmacy and chemistry. Tuition was fifty-five dollars a term, and room and board cost a dollar fifty a week. While at medical school, her sweetheart was Mr. Albert Miller.

She became a doctor at the age of twenty-two in June 1855; she was the only woman in her class. She launched her career in Columbus, Ohio. Ohioans did not want a woman doctor, so she went to Rome, New York. She did not have much better success there. People were put off because she wore bloomers, and folks thought her a militant feminist.

Bloomers
Dr. Walker's outfits were very similar to this one

She and Dr. Miller were married at her parents' home. She wore trousers and a dress coat (remember, this was the mid-1850s), and the "obey" part of the vows was eliminated. She kept her maiden name.

They both had medical offices, and things went fine for a while. Then, she separated from him when he admitted to being unfaithful. She was not doing well at all financially; her office was now above a clothing store. She concentrated on treating women and children, but she also saw the occasional male patient.

She lectured robustly for dress reform. She decried the tight and cumbersome clothes women wore. She also found time to plead for the establishment of a New York state foundling hospital.

In the late summer of 1860, she went to Iowa for a divorce. Now twenty-seven years old, she stayed there for a few months. Back in Rome in the late spring of 1861, she had not gotten a divorce after all (it would eventually go through in 1869).

Still in bloomers, she went to Washington, D.C. after the Battle of Bull Run. She made herself useful wherever she was needed. Her application for a commission as an army surgeon was rejected. The Surgeon General, it seems, did not want a woman doctor.

She volunteered at a makeshift hospital set up in the United States Patent Office. There, she worked as an assistant physician and surgeon, but she was not on the payroll. During the coming months, she was a hospital administrator. She also counseled lonely, wounded soldiers. She sometimes accompanied wounded soldiers to their out-of-state, faraway homes. She helped secure hundreds of checkerboards for Washington hospitals to help bored patients while away long hours.

Alarmed at the many amputations taking place, she often convinced soldiers to refuse to have limbs amputated. She was instrumental in having a house established for women and children who came to Washington to visit hospitalized menfolk. When the house originally made available proved inadequate, she made her own home available.

She went to New York for another medical degree in 1862 and returned to Washington that autumn. She was present at the Battle of Fredericksburg. In the spring of 1863, she attended a Rochester annual convention of the Reform-Dress Society where she was elected a vice-president.

On April 10, 1864, she became a prisoner of war of the Confederate States of America Army. She was taken to Georgia, then on to Richmond. Curious throngs turned out at various stops along the way to see the bloomered physician. She was incarcerated at Castle Thunder, a political prison. She was exchanged as a surgeon two months later for a major in the Confederate Army.

On October 5, 1864, she was named Acting Assistant Surgeon of the U.S. Army with pay of one hundred dollars a month. Her first assignment was as Surgeon in the Women's Prison Hospital in Louisville. She was there for six months then grew bored and requested transfer to the fighting front.

She was sent to Tennessee and placed in charge of an orphanage. She was also responsible for refugee families living in the area. It seems she was not to go to where the fighting was.

Her war service ended in mid-June 1865, and she was in Richmond three weeks later. On January 24, 1866, she became the first woman to receive the Congressional Medal of Honor. She wore it proudly until her death, as well as a replacement with a modified design. In 1917, the Board of Medal Awards ruled the award was unjustified and demanded she return it. She refused, as one might well imagine.

After the War, she stayed in Washington where she practiced medicine with moderate success. In June of 1866, she was elected president of the National Dress Reform Movement. That fall, she went to Manchester, England as a rights delegate to a social science congress; the topic was suffrage. Her bloomers caught the press's eye, and she made news throughout her United Kingdom stay.

She lectured during her stay -- her first lecture was at St. James' Hall to a packed room. She spoke about her life, her medical practice and her war experiences. Reviews were good, and she was soon well booked; she also lectured in Scotland.

She had been abroad a year when she returned to Washington, D.C. She embarked on a short, unsuccessful lecture tour. As the years since the War lengthened, people were less interested in hearing about war exploits. She went out West and lectured with very moderate success.

Casting about for ways to drum up money on which to live, she completed an autobiography entitled, Hit. The book contained chapters on love and marriage, dress reform, tobacco and temperance. Seven years later, she published Unmasked, or the Science of Immorality which contained discussions of sex -- kissing, hermaphrodites, hymens, seminal weakness. In spite of such scintillating topics (or perhaps because of), the book was by no means a bestseller.

She made Washington her command center where she was prominent in women's rights. She also spent time in Oswego. During the War, she received an eye injury for which she was awarded eight dollars and fifty cents a month. She applied for a larger pension of twenty-four dollars a month, but her request was denied. In 1980, she would finally be awarded a pension of twenty dollars a month in addition to her injury pension.

She wanted a position in the Federal government and got one in the mailroom of the Pensions Office in 1882. She now had a regular income after a decade of knocking around in a hardscrabble existence. Never one to play well with other children, she was on the verge of being fired less than a year later. She took a leave of absence and went to Oswego. There, she received word that she was discharged. She fought to get her job back but lost.

In 1887, she hit the lecture circuit again appearing as one of several acts at sideshows in dime museums. She filled several Midwest engagements, earning a princely one hundred and fifty dollars a week. In 1893 at the age of sixty-one, she filled bookings in Detroit and Buffalo.

Dr. Walker must have been gratified in the mid-1890s as bloomers and split skirts were seen as bicycling became all the rage. It was the start, fueled by Dr. Walker and the dress-reform movement, of a widespread change in dress. Soon, women would gladly wave goodbye to hot, cumbersome and constrictive clothing.

In the early 1890s, Dr. Walker was spending more time in Oswego. She had received title to the mortgaged family farm with her late father's stipulation that she look after her mother. She fought with her brother Alvah who lived next door, and she drove her tenants away. She lived in New York half the year.

She traveled to Washington, D.C. to watch Congress in session, and she traveled around the Northeast. The mundane running of the farm was left to others, and tenant farmers never stayed long. She was in danger of losing the farm because there was not enough money to pay taxes. Her older sister helped her out financially.

Now old, Dr. Walker spent more time on the farm. She sold butter, vegetables and berries in town to help make ends meet. Was she enjoying a boring, docile old age? Not hardly.

Still a firecracker, in 1897 she addressed a Washington crowd of two thousand at the first Congress of Mothers. This congress would later become the National Congress of Parents and Teachers. She made pilgrimages most years to Albany on behalf of women's suffrage.

In April 1917, she sent a cablegram to Kaiser Wilhelm asking him to stop World War I. She offered her farm as a site for a peace conference. There was no response from the Kaiser. That war would see a major revolution in women's clothing. With the men off to war, women filled factory jobs and lifted their hemlines. Pants were sometimes worn for safety in factory work. Housewives soon followed suit.

Dr. Walker deeded the farm to a favorite nephew. Growing ill at the age of eighty-six, she entered the hospital. She left a few weeks later and went home. She was cared for by a kindly neighbor until her death on February 21, 1919. She was buried in her black suit in the family plot.

Thus ended the interesting life of a unique woman. So it would seem. However, Dr. Walker would not give up the limelight so easily! In 1982, a twenty cents stamp honoring her was issued. It commemorated her as the first woman to receive the Congressional Medal of Honor (which had been reinstated posthumously in 1977), and as the second woman to graduate from a United States medical school.

Oak Alley Plantation
Vacherie, Louisiana

Oak Alley Plantation was built in 1836 by Mr. Jacques Roman and his wife, Celina. The Roman family were French Creole, and it was a distinguished family. Mr. Andre Roman, brother of Mr. Jacques, was a two-time governor of Louisiana. Their sister, Miss Josephine, was married to Mr. Francois Gabriel Aimee, "The Sugar King of Louisiana".

The veranda extends thirteen feet from the front porch walls, helping to shade the house from Louisiana's intense summer heat. Special care was given to the gardens when the house was designed. Miss Celina Roman, legend has it, christened the house "Bon Sojourn" (pleasant journey). Travelers on the Mississippi River, greatly impressed by the majestic oaks, called it "Oak Alley".

The Roman family resided at Oak Alley during the Civil War; Mr. Roman had died in 1848. His son Henri overtook the business running of the plantation in 1859. He was forced to sell it in 1866, ending thirty years of living at Oak Alley for the Romans.

Mr. Antoine Sorrel, a Portuguese native and Confederate veteran, purchased Oak Alley in 1881. It flourished, and he lived there for twenty-four years. In 1905, advancing years and declining health convinced him to sell it. The new owners left after a year or so, and the beautiful house was boarded up.

In 1917, Mr. Jefferson Davis Hardin, Jr. wanted to transform Oak Alley into a model farm run by scientific methods. The house and gardens benefited from the care of his wife and daughters. After seven years, however, Mr. Hardin's experiment failed because of fires, floods and problems with livestock. He signed Oak Alley over to a bank, and the great house was still once more.

In 1925, the Andrew Stewarts purchased Oak Alley and undertook a massive restoration effort. Now restored to its former glory, the mansion is open for tours.

Abolitionists

The abolition or anti-slavery movement took firm root in the early 1830s. Formerly, the movement had championed the gradual end of slavery through prohibiting it in the territories. Then the face of abolition changed, and an immediate end to slavery was the mission to be touted.

In 1832, the Northeast Anti-Slavery Society was set up; this began a beginning of organization for the movement. In 1833, Messrs. Arthur and Lewis Tappan formed a similar group; these men took the lead in starting a national society.

The American Anti-Slavery Society conceded that each state had a right to legislate on its domestic institutions. No one was trying to tell the states what to do. The Society, however, set a goal of convincing fellow citizens that slavery was a heinous crime that should be immediately abandoned.

The Grimke sisters helped to bring women into the anti-slavery movement in the 1840s. They were daughters of a prominent South Carolina family; the sisters moved North to embrace anti-slavery and feminism. Miss Angelina Grimke published Appeal to the Christian

<u>Women of the South</u> in 1836; she wanted Southern women to speak and act against slavery.

African-Americans were quite active in the anti-slavery movement. They were often former slaves who could speak from sad, first-hand experience on the horrors of slavery.

Susan B. Anthony

Miss Susan B. Anthony was born in 1820 in Massachusetts to a Quaker family. She taught school for fifteen years, then she became active in temperance. She joined the women's rights movement in 1852 and decided to make her life's work women's suffrage.

After moving to Rochester, New York, members of her family became staunch abolitionists. She became an agent for the American Anti-Slavery Society in 1856. She arranged meetings, made speeches, and distributed leaflets.

She encountered much opposition to her anti-slavery efforts -- she was hung in effigy, and her image was dragged through the streets of Syracuse. In 1863, she and Miss Elizabeth Cady Stanton, wife of Secretary of War Edwin Stanton, got their heads together. They organized a Women's National Loyal League to petition for the Thirteenth Amendment which would outlaw slavery. Miss Anthony campaigned for equal rights for all people in her newspaper, The Revolution; she began publishing it in 1868.

After the War, she tried to establish trade schools for female printers. In the 1890s, she was president of the National American Women Suffrage Association, and she emphasized the importance of organized labor. She supported the Rochester women organizers of the Women's Christian Temperance Union in the 1870s.

In 1866, she and Miss Stanton founded the American Equal Rights Association. The suffrage movement split in 1869 -- Miss Anthony's group wanted a constitutional amendment, whereas another group campaigned for getting women the vote on a state-by-state basis.

Miss Anthony, three of her sisters and other women were arrested for voting in Rochester in 1872 before women had the vote. She was ordered to pay a one hundred dollar fine which she refused to do. The judge did not imprison her.

The two suffrage groups merged in 1887 to become the National American Woman Suffrage Association. Miss Stanton was president, and Miss Anthony was vice-president. She became president in 1892 when Miss Stanton retired.

Miss Anthony retired in 1900 at the age of eighty. In 1904, she presided over the International Council of Women in Berlin. She also became honorary president of Miss Carrie Chapman Catt's International Woman Suffrage Alliance.

Miss Anthony died in 1906 in Rochester. With the Ninth Amendment, women got the vote in 1920. This amendment is also known as the Susan B. Anthony Amendment.

Harriet Beecher Stowe

Miss Harriet Beecher Stowe is one of the best known abolitionists. Born in 1811 in Connecticut, she was the daughter of a famous Congregationalist minister. She was educated at the Hartford Female Academy, where she later taught. She also taught at the Western Female Institute in Cincinnati.

In 1836, she married widower Mr. Calvin Stowe, and they had seven children. Miss Stowe wrote magazine articles, poems, children's novels and ten adult novels. She is known mainly for her first adult novel, Uncle Tom's Cabin published in 1852. The well-written, dramatic novel focused on the issue of slavery and how it adversely affected the lives of slaves.

Miss Howe became a celebrity because of the book. She lectured widely in America and in Europe. Uncle Tom's Cabin has never been out of print and in the years preceding the Civil War, it opened the world's eyes to slavery.

She published a second anti-slavery novel in 1856, Dred. She wrote A Key to Uncle Tom's Cabin in 1853 which detailed the realities on which Uncle Tom's Cabin was based. This book was written to quiet detractors who insisted that the events portrayed in Uncle Tom's Cabin could not possibly have been true.

In 1867, the Stowes bought thirty acres in northeast Florida which became their winter home until the winter of 1883-84. They moved to Florida both for philanthropic efforts among African-Americans and because of their son's poor health. While in Florida, Miss Stowe wrote sketches called "Palmetto Leaves". She died in 1896.

Sojourner Truth (Isabella Baumfree)

Miss Isabella Baumfree was born in 1797 in upstate New York. She was born to slave parents in a Dutch settlement. She spoke only Dutch until she was sold at the age of eleven. Her new master was cruel, and she learned quickly to speak English.

She was sold many times, but her strong Christian faith helped see her through the hardness of her life. Her third owner forced her to marry an older slave named Thomas, and they had five children. New York ended slavery in 1828. When her owner reneged on his promise to free her a year before the emancipation, she fled with her infant son.

She settled in New York City and worked as a domestic for several religious communities. In 1843, she had a religious revelation that changed her life. She changed her name to "Sojourner Truth" and preached salvation throughout Long Island and Connecticut.

She arrived in Massachusetts and joined the utopian community "The Northampton Association for Education and Industry". There, she meet well-known abolitionists Messrs. William Lloyd Garrison and Frederick Douglass. She published her memoirs in 1850, <u>The Narrative of Sojourner Truth: A Northern Slave</u>. Undoubtedly, her memoirs did much to open the country's eyes to the issue of slavery.

She lectured about abolitionism and suffrage, often giving personal testimony about her life as a slave. Miss Truth spoke at an Ohio women's convention in 1851 and her phrase, "Ain't I a Woman" was associated with her after this speech.

She worked to aid newly freed slaves when the War was over, and she attempted to petition Congress to give former slaves land in the West. Miss Truth died in 1883 in Michigan.

Harriet Tubman

Miss Harriet Ross was born in Dorchester County, Maryland. She and both parents were slaves. At the age of twelve, she suffered a serious head injury inflicted by a white overseer. At age twenty-five, she married free man Mr. John Tubman.

She escaped when she was thirty, fearing she would be sold South. Her escape would prove to be convoluted: a white neighbor gave her a paper and told her how to find the first house on the path to freedom. There, she was hidden in a wagon and driven to her next destination. In Philadelphia, she met Mr. William Still, Philadelphia stationmaster on the Underground Railroad. She appreciated its usefulness now that she had successfully escaped. Consequently, she learned how the Underground Railroad worked, and she decided she would use it to free as many slaves as possible.

The Underground Railroad (UGRR) had general routes of escape from the Deep South into Illinois, Indiana and Ohio, from Tennessee and Georgia toward Washington, D.C. and Delaware, and from the Carolinas to Boston and Maine. Many slaves went on to Canada, and some went to the Caribbean.

To get to the North, many, many miles

of walking, usually under cover of darkness, was necessary. It was a nerve racking process at best, a dangerous one at worst. No slave wanted to be captured and sent back, because their fate would be uncertain and sometimes tragic. Masters did not take kindly to slaves who tried to escape.

African-Americans and sympathetic whites worked together closely, and most runaways began their arduous journey on their own. The abolitionist movement expanded the network and helped to publicize it. The UGRR existed openly in the North, and it simmered beneath the surface in the South.

In 1851, Miss Tubman began relocating her family to Ontario. She stayed there until 1857, using Ontario as her home base. She was truly the "Moses" of slaves, leading them to hopeful new lives. Slaves knew they could trust her to have their best interests at heart. She went back to her home state of Maryland to organize escapes nineteen times.

Many people are surprised that Marylanders owned slaves because Maryland was in the Union. The state is south of the Mason-Dixon line which is the delineation point between North and South. By all rights, it should have stayed firmly in the South. Maryland reluctantly became a border state because President Lincoln could not afford to have Washington, D.C., the capital of the Union, in enemy territory. He rounded up Maryland's pro-Confederate leaders and tossed them in jail. With those leaders out of the way, the fall elections returned a solidly Unionist majority to the state.

Miss Tubman was believed to have conducted an astonishing three hundred people to freedom. She threatened to shoot frightened people who wanted to turn back. She was not being cruel or heartless when she made this threat. She felt they might inadvertently tell the wrong people about secret escape routes; then the safety of others would be endangered. She was fearless, calm and level-headed; she did whatever was necessary to achieve success. She often put her own life at risk in order to bring others to freedom.

She purchased the Auburn, New York home of Governor William Seward and used it as her base of operations. She was also a soldier, a spy and a nurse in the Civil War. She became a Federal espionage agent in 1862, and she served as a spy and a scout for about a year. She served her country well, and she did not seem to be afraid of new challenges. It seems the intrepid woman was not too busy for romance; during her war work, she met Mr. Nelson Davis, ten years her junior.

She apparently liked upstate New York. At War's end, she returned to Auburn, married Mr. Davis and built a house. Still aiming to help others, she was active in supporting women's rights. In 1908, the kind-hearted woman built a home for the aged and indigent. She worked there and died there in 1913.

Miss Tubman's humanitarian efforts would not go unrecognized by the United States Government. In 1944, the Liberty Ship Harriet Tubman was christened by

Eleanor Roosevelt. Then in 1995, Miss Tubman was forever honored with a commemorative postage stamp portraying her name and likeness.

Hampton Mansion
Towson, Maryland

Destrehan Plantation
Destrehan, Louisiana

Destrehan Plantation, twenty miles from New Orleans, is the oldest documented plantation house in the lower Mississippi River Valley. In 1787, Mr. Robin deLogny built a French Colonial style house.

In 1810, daughter Celeste and her husband, Mr. Jean Noel d'Estrehan purchased the plantation. They added two wings to accommodate their fourteen children. Daughters lived in the house after their parents' deaths in the early 1820s.

In 1840, owners Louise and Judge

Pierre Rost remodeled the house to Greek Revival. The Rost family were in Europe in 1861 when the Union Army seized the house and established the Rost Home Colony. The Colony operated under control of the Freedman's Bureau, and newly freed slaves learned trades.

After the War ended, the Rosts got their house back and lived there until their deaths. Son Emile then purchased the property. Family ownership ended in 1910 when the property was sold to the Destrehan Planting and Manufacturing Company. Ownership changed many times through the years until 1958 when owner American Oil Company left the site.

The house sat abandoned for twelve years at the mercy of vandals who stole everything of value. Legends of hidden treasure led to interior walls being ripped out. Local citizens formed the River Road Historical Society to save the house from ruin. In 1971, the house and four acres were deeded to the Society.

The house has been tenderly restored. Docents dressed in period costumes lead daily tours, and demonstrations of period crafts enable visitors to witness the ways plantations worked.

Mary Chesnut

Writing in journals and diaries has been a pleasant and often productive pastime for many women almost since the beginning of time. Some women have turned journal scribblings into full-fledged books of both fiction and non-fiction. Mary Boykin Miller Chesnut, born in South Carolina to a future governor, wrote the definitive diary of the Civil War. She was a gentlewoman of society, well-born and high bred.

At the age of seventeen, she married Mr. James Chesnut in 1840. He was the surviving son of one of South Carolina's largest landowners. They spent most of the following twenty years at his plantation. He became a senator in 1858. At that point, the Chesnuts traded their tranquil planter's life in the country for one of parties and excitement in the glittering city of Washington, D.C.

They became friends with the Jefferson Davises. She and Miss Davis grew close, and they enjoyed social activities together on many happy occasions. Miss Davis was a rather serious minded individual who tended to take herself too seriously, whereas Miss Chesnut was more a life of the party type. The two personality types seemed to balance each other out. Miss Davis knew firsthand how upset Miss Chesnut was at being childless.

After Mr. Lincoln's election to the Presidency, the Chesnuts resolutely returned to South Carolina. They wished to help affect their state's secession. South Carolina was the first state to secede.

Mr. Chesnut became a general in the Confederate States of America's Army. Miss Chesnut accompanied him to Charleston, Montgomery, Columbia and Richmond. Her drawing rooms were coveted salons for the Confederate elite, and she was privy to many military discussions.

Miss Chesnut dutifully wrote her diary on a day-to-day basis from 1860-1865. She told of the making of the Confederate constitution, and she spoke of a continuing gaiety in the midst of onerous war talk. Southerners realized that trouble was coming, but they continued about their happy lives. What else could they do?

She spoke glowingly of sparkling dinner parties, and she somewhat playfully compared bouquets of flowers she received. Realizing the Confederacy was in a calm before the storm, she was quite the social butterfly. She flitted all around genteel Charleston in the company of lively, engaging companions.

She grew quite serious, however, as she described watching the Battle of Fort Sumter from a housetop. People could no longer doubt that the war was coming. Her dress caught on fire when she unknowingly sat on a rooftop chimney in the darkness as the opening battle of the War Between the States raged before her eyes.

She wrote of all the major battles of the War -- Manassas, Shiloh, the Monitor and the Virginia, Vicksburg, Antietam, Gettysburg. She spoke (not favorably) about Sherman at Atlanta. She wrote copiously about Richmond's many troubles. Also on her mind were conscription, slavery -- at one point she described the distressing sight of seeing a woman sold on the auction block, and hardships imposed by the blockades. She pointed out that some gourmet foods and fine wines slipped through the blockades when the War was young (she apparently liked a fine meal).

She talked of engagements and weddings. At one wedding, the bridesmaid wore black widow's weeds for her husband who had fallen in battle. The woman knelt at the altar throughout the subdued ceremony, overcome with grief. The bride wore her mourning bridesmaid's wedding dress -- white satin with delicate, exquisite lace. The wedding guests hoped that the bride's handsome soldier husband would not suffer the same fate as that of the bridesmaid's young man.

At another happier wedding in the middle of the War, the bride's dress was crafted from crisp white muslin originally meant to be used for curtains. The wedding did not suffer in the least -- laughter and gaiety rang throughout the day. Guests were dressed in their best finery (even if some of it *had* seen better days -- the blockades were not making it easy to get good fabrics).

Miss Chesnut also wrote of budding romances, some of which seemed rather

unlikely.   But then Cupid's arrow is
sometimes blind and deaf!   Miss Chesnut
was very likely something of a matchmaker.

She   spoke   impressively   of   writers
George Elliott and William Thackeray and
Miss Robert E. Lee and her daughters.
Miss Chesnut liked nothing better than to
receive   the   company   of   educated,
intelligent people.

She described the March 1865 exodus
from Richmond and the fall of Richmond as
General Lee retreated.   There seemed to be
little bitterness in her writing as she
talked about these subjects.   She was
objective and seemed intent on describing
events   as   vividly   and   accurately   as
possible.

After the War, the Chesnuts returned
to South Carolina to rebuild their lives.
Miss Mary Chesnut wrote three novels which
were never published.   In the 1880s at the
suggestion of her enchanted friends, she
expanded her war diaries.   She called her
effort A Diary From Dixie.   The book was
not published until 1904, and it was then
called   Mary Chesnut's Civil War.   Miss
Chesnut died on November 22, 1886.

Miss   Mary   Chesnut's   diary   is   an
amazing read for anyone who desires a
detailed, lively look at life during and
immediately after the Civil War.

Julia Ward Howe

Born in 1819 in New York City, Miss Julia Ward grew liberal on religion and social issues despite her Calvinist upbringing. At twenty-one years of age, she married reformer Mr. Samuel Gridley Howe, director of the Perkins Institute for the Blind in Boston. Although he married her for her mind and for her commitment to causes he shared, he did not want his wife to have any life outside the home.

The Howes and their six children lived on the Perkins campus, and Miss Howe lived in isolation. She was allowed to attend a Unitarian church. She wrote poetry, and she kept a diary that indicated the marriage was violent. She considered divorce from her controlling, unfaithful husband, but divorce in that time was a difficult affair. Besides, where could she go with no money? Plus, she would be cut off from her children -- divorce in those days strongly favored husbands.

She studied philosophy, learned several languages and continued to write. She published poems and plays. Her success angered her resentful husband even more.

During the War, husband and wife became volunteers in the United States Sanitary Commission. The organization sought to improve conditions in military camps in order to prevent disease. President Lincoln invited them to Washington, D.C. because of their work with the Sanitary Commission. There, Miss Howe heard men signing a song about Mr. John Brown's death. She could not get the song out of her mind.

Inspired, she wrote a poem, "Battle Hymn of the Republic". It was published in the February 1862 issue of Atlantic Monthly, and she was paid five dollars. The poem was soon set to the tune used for "John Brown's Body". The result became the North's best known Civil War song.

Miss Howe was often asked to speak publicly, and her husband's resentment thawed a bit. She worked with soldiers' widows and orphans and was appalled at the unseen effects of war. In 1870, she wanted women to band together to commit to finding peaceful resolutions to conflicts. Nothing came of her attempt to get recognition for a Mother's Day of Peace, but her efforts are a part of history.

Jennie Wade

Miss Jennie Wade awoke that morning with a gentle smile and tender thoughts of her handsome sweetheart, Corporal Johnston Skelly, on her mind. Folks knew that she and the soldier from the 87th Pennsylvania would marry. Twenty-year-old Miss Wade was looking forward to making her own home -- her own furniture, curtains and dishes.

She and her mother were visiting her sister. It was going to be very hot this July 3, 1863, so Miss Wade went downstairs early to start her day's work. Born as Mary Virginia, she had somehow come to be called Jennie. Now before the sun started to swelter, she began the task of baking bread for hungry Union troops.

It seemed that everyone was on edge these days as the Battle of Gettysburg raged nearby -- much too close for comfort as far as Miss Wade was concerned. Her sister's house was almost in the backyard of the battle!

The fierce battle had happened by accident. General Lee thought he could weaken the Union Army if fighting moved to Northern soil. He dragged his army through Virginia's lush Shenandoah Valley, then through Maryland. Rebel soldiers innocently entered the town of Gettysburg hoping to find shoes. Instead, they found trouble when they encountered Union

soldiers.   General   Lee's   battle   for
victory on Northern soil would take place
in Miss Wade's pleasant town.

Battlefield
Gettysburg, Pennsylvania

Humming   to   herself,   Miss   Wade
assembled the needed ingredients and began
the tedious bread-making process. She did
not mind the hot, time-consuming work.
She imagined some other woman might be
doing the same for her sweetheart's unit.

Wiping sweat from her brow, she felt
a sharp, hot sting on her back and briefly
wondered if an insect had bitten her.
Then she slumped to the floor, dead from a
stray bullet that had entered the house in
a bizarre twist of fate.

Miss Jennie Wade was the only
civilian killed in a bloody, three-day
battle that would claim fifty thousand
lives. Tragically, her young sweetheart
died in another battle.

Everywoman

There were many unsung heroines of the Civil War -- women who led quiet, ordinary lives. They were then, as now, divided among class lines -- upper class, middle class and lower class. What were their lives like during this ghastliest of wars?

Upper class women lived in large houses -- plantations in the South, mansions or very large farms in the North. Their husbands were planters, large-scale farmers, lawyers, doctors, editors or factory owners.

In the South, members of this class perceived themselves as community leaders; they thought their way of living was one that others should emulate. They were much like English gentry or country gentlemen and gentlewomen. Their Northern counterparts were equally snooty -- certain that lesser folks envied them their wealth and status.

Women of this class were usually accomplished in some way -- perhaps they played the piano or the harp, perhaps they sketched or dabbled in watercolors, perhaps they wrote poetry or kept journals, or maybe they did intricate needlework. Their accomplishments were spotlighted to acknowledge their finishing school education.

Their job was to oversee the runnings of their house. They supervised slaves or servants, they saw to it that the kitchen ran smoothly, and they sometimes took care of the sick. Their children's education was very important, and they oversaw their efforts and progress in this regard. The children went on to higher education -- college for the boys, and finishing school (or sometimes a female academy) for the girls.

The upper class woman was expected to entertain frequently and lavishly. One of her primary roles was to support her husband in his business endeavors. These wives had to have a superficial knowledge of current events and politics in order to take part in dinner conversations. They usually had a knowledge of history and literature as well.

These women dressed very well in the latest fashions from England and Paris. The fabrics of their clothing were the very best; no expense was spared. What good was it to be wealthy if others could not see it? Average women eyed them with envy and speculation about what it must be like to live such lives of splendor.

The middle class woman could be the wife of an overseer, a spouse of a small farm owner or perhaps the wife of a shop owner. Their houses were much smaller than those of the upper class. There were no slaves or servants about, except perhaps for the occasional hired hands.

These women did their own housework, plus they often helped their husbands in the fields or in the shops. These women could afford to dress fairly well. There were none of the latest frills and fashions, nor were they running around in rags. In rural areas, women usually made their own clothes.

Middle class women of both the North and South had lives that were full of hard work, but they got by. They enjoyed their families, and their goal was to ensure that their children would have a better life. The children usually did not go beyond a basic public school education, although the boys often learned a trade.

Poor women had a thoroughly rough time of it. If married to farmers, their land would be the least desirable -- full of rocks or with poor soil. The farm would be very small, and the family would likely be renting the land. Most of them would not have the means to buy land. This class lived on the fringes of society, and these folks kept to themselves. There would have been little reason to go to town since they could not afford to buy anything.

They were lethargic and did not take kindly to work; dietary deficiencies were probably the culprits. Without good nutrition, the body cannot function with optimum results. These folks somehow managed to scratch out a subsistence farming living. In urban areas, they might do odd jobs to bring in much needed cash. They did whatever they could to get by.

Whatever their status in life, these women helped to get our nation through the War. They all waited patiently and hopefully for their soldiers to come home from the War. When their men failed to appear, these women all wept bitter tears. When their men returned home physically or mentally different, these women dealt with that situation.

These women faced the challenges imposed by the War Between the States with stoicism. Their names or actions will never be found in the records of history. Nevertheless, their everyday actions and lives were every bit as important as those of the most famous women.

Boone Hall Plantation
Mt. Pleasant, South Carolina

Boone Hall Plantation, quite near Charleston, is one of the South's oldest working plantations. It was established in 1681 by Major John Boone who came to the New World from England that year. At that time, the lush grounds covered seventeen thousand acres; they now encompass over seven hundred acres.

Upon entering the plantation gates, the stately Avenue of Oaks, planted by Captain John Boone, the founder's son, leads to the mansion. Legend has it that Captain Boone's life may have ended prematurely and tragically on the Avenue. He was thrown from his frightened horse as he thundered down the Avenue to welcome his visiting fiancé to Boone Hall.

The dock house is on the banks of Wampancheone Creek. Cotton bales were loaded on barges and floated out to Charleston Harbor. From there, they went to the spinning mills up North and in England. Bricks produced from creek mud are seen in all the brick structures on the grounds.

The house is listed in the National Register of Historic Places. During its glory days, Boone Hall Plantation was the center of high society, fashionable parties and political events.

The plantation was rebuilt in 1934 by Mr. Thomas Stone, replacing the original house. All the brickwork was completed by using bricks from the old house and handmade bricks found in storage.

Boone Hall is known as America's most photographed plantation. It currently grows a variety of fruits, Christmas trees and colorful flowers. Tours of the plantation are conducted by costumed hostesses, and visitors can leisurely stroll the gardens.

Bibliography

Randall, Ruth Painter. Mary Lincoln ---
Biography of a Marriage. Boston:
Little Brown & Company, 1953

Ross, Ishbel. The First Lady of the
South: The Life of Mrs. Jefferson
Davis. New York, Harper & Brothers
Publishers, 1958

http://www.cojoweb.com/malinda blaylock.ht
ml. "Women That Served in the Civil War as
Soldiers"

http://www.civilwarhome.com/edmondsbio.htm
"Sara Emma Edmonds Biography Page"

http://cabinet.editthispage.com/stories/St
oryReader$1072, "Amazon of the Month:
Jennie Hodgers"

Leonard, Elizabeth D. All The Daring of
the Soldier: Women of the Civil War
Armies. New York: W.W. Norton &
Comapny, 1999 (Loreta Velezquez)

http://www.sandiego.edu/~kelliej/wakeman.h
tml, "Sarah Rosetta Wakeman"

http://www.buffalosoldiers.com/CathayWilli
ams.com, "Buffalo Soldiers - Cathay
Williams, Female Buffalo Soldier"

http://www2.shore.net/~sbl/colorbearer.htm
(Kady Brownell)

Leonard, Elizabeth D. Ibid. (Bridget
Divers, Annie Etheridge, Belle
Reynolds, Nadine Turchin)
Turchin)

wysiwyg://53/http://www.lkwdpl.org/wihohio
/bows-mar.htm, "Mary Elizabeth Bowser
Biography"

Leonard, Elizabeth D. Ibid. (Belle Boyd)

http://www.civilwarhome.com/boydbio.htm,
"Belle Boyd Biography"

Bibliography

http://Civilwar.bluegrass.net/Spie..rsAnd
Partisans/paulinecushman.html

http://users.erols.com/kfraser/fairfax/
Antonia.html, "Who Was Antonia Ford?"

Ross, Ishbel. Rebel Rose -- Life of Rose
O'Neal Greenhow, Confederate Spy,
Marietta, Georgia: Mockingbird Books,
1973

http://www.nkclifton.com/nancy.html,
"Nancy Hart Story"

http://userpages.aug.com/captbarb/moon.
html, "Confederate Sister Act -- The
Moon Sister Spies"

http://thecivilwar.netfirms.com/women/
w3-thompson.htm, "Sarah E. Thompson"

Leonard, Elizabeth D. Ibid.
(Elizabeth Van Lew)

Ross, Ishbel. The Life of Clara Barton.
New York: Harper and Brothers
Publishers, 1956

http://www.civilwarhome.com/dixbio.htm,
"Dorothea Dix Biography"

http://www.jewish history.com/Pember/,
"Phoebe Yates Pember"

http://historymaters.gmu.edu/d/6599/
"Susie King Taylor Assists the First
South Carolina Volunteers, 1862-1864

wysiwyg://70http://women history..om//
library/prm/blcaptainsally.htm, "Sally
Louisa Tompkins -- Captain Sally"

Snyder, Charles McCool. Dr. Mary Walker --
The Little Lady in Pants. New York:
Arno Press, 1974

http://www.susanbanthonyhouse.org/
biography.html

http://digital.library.upenn.edu/women/
Stowe/Stowe.HB.html

Bibliography

wysiwyg://12/http://ww.lkwdpl.org/
wihohio/trut_soj.htm, "Sojourner Truth
Biography"

http://www.nyhistory.com/harriettubman/
life.htm, "The Life of Harriet Tubman"

http://www.cr.nps.gov/nr/travel/under-
ground/ugrrintr.htm

http://education.ucddavis.edu/NEW/STC/
lesson/socstud/railroad/Map.htm

http://docsouth.unc.edu/chesnut/about.
html, "About Mary Boykin Chesnut"

wysiwyg://10http://womenshistory.about.
com/library/weekly/aa013100a.htm,
"Julia Ward Howe--The Early Years--
Beyond the Battle Hymn of the Republic"

http://arar.essortment.com/jenniewade
psx.htm

http://july1863.homestead.com/jenniewade.
html/

Shi, David E. and Tindall, George Brown.
America: A Narrative History Volume
One. New York: W.W. Norton and
Company, 1984

Index

Darlene Funkhouser spent part of her childhood in Virginia's Shenandoah Valley, where her parents were born and raised. She holds degrees in Law Enforcement and Business Management, and she is a former police reserve officer. A reporter for a local newspaper while still in high school, she once had a Hollywood screenplay agent. She is the author of <u>Civil War Cookin', Stories 'n Such</u>. She lives in Florida.

To Order Copies

    Please send me _____ copies of *Women of the Civil War* at **$9.95** each plus **$3.00** S/H. (Make checks payable to **QUIXOTE PRESS.**)

Name _____

Street _____

City _____ State _____ Zip _____

Quixote Press
3544 Blakslee Street
Wever, IA 52658
1-800-571-2665

To Order Copies

    Please send me _____ copies of *Women of the Civil War* at **$9.95** each plus **$3.00** S/H. (Make checks payable to **QUIXOTE PRESS.**)

Name _____

Street _____

City _____ State _____ Zip _____

Quixote Press
3544 Blakslee Street
Wever, IA 52658
1-800-571-2665